STEPHEN KING'S MAINE

STEPHEN KING'S MAINE

A History & Guide

Sharon Kitchens

THE
History
PRESS

Published by The History Press
Charleston, SC
www.historypress.com

Front cover, top: The Bridgton location of Reny's, a chain of department stores located throughout Maine. Photo taken sometime in the early 1960s. *Courtesy of the Bridgton Historical Society*; *bottom*: Stephen King's former home in Bangor. *Photo by author.*
Back cover: Main Street, Lisbon Falls, 1963. The local egg delivery man is leaning against his blue truck. *Courtesy of the Lisbon Falls Historical Society.*

First published 2024

Manufactured in the United States

ISBN 9781467157148

Library of Congress Control Number: 2024931542

Notice: The information in this book is true and complete to the best of our knowledge. It is offered without guarantee on the part of the author or The History Press. The author and The History Press disclaim all liability in connection with the use of this book.

Statewide map of towns included in this book. *Illustration by author.*

CONTENTS

WATCH YOUR STEP, PLEASE!

This book is intended to be read with the knowledge that many of the places mentioned are private property or are otherwise legally off-limits and as such cannot be visited without permission, if at all. Trips to any of the locations featured in this book are undertaken as a personal choice of the reader and not at the instigation of the author. Sharon Kitchens does not support trespassing, lawbreaking or acts of vandalism of any kind.

ACKNOWLEDGEMENTS

Faulkner and Tennessee
Hayley Barton, Portland Museum of Art
Geremy Chubbuck, University of Maine
Joshua Clifford
Mike Davis, Bridgton Historical Society
Anne Marie, Danielle and Roland Demers
Dorris and Doug Hall
Ron Huston
Jennifer Madigan, The Public Theatre
Emilio Millan
Timothy Morey
Margaret Nagle, University of Maine
Desiree Butterfield-Nagy, University of Maine
The Portland Public Library
Dorothy and Alfred Smith, Lisbon Historical Society
Michelle Souliere, Green Hand Bookshop
Hannah Wilber
Earl Williams, Lisbon Historical Society
Monica Willis

INTRODUCTION

didn't know I was moving to Maine until I did. In Los Angeles, California, about twenty years ago, I set off with a friend on a cross-country road trip. Somewhere in MidCoast Maine would be the turnaround point. We took the southern route across the country, visiting the stockyards in the Texas Panhandle city of Amarillo, the cocktail bars and psychics of the Big Easy and the Civil Rights Memorial Center in Alabama's capital, and in Boston we caught a live show and dropped into a few of Newbury Street's chic boutiques.

As I sat on a bench by the harbormaster's shack in Camden, Maine, looking out at the kayakers and schooners in one of the most picturesque towns I'd ever been in, unburdened and free, I decided to stay. I'd signed up for a weeklong photography class at the Maine Media Workshops in neighboring Rockport and picked up a few books at the local independent bookshop the Owl and Turtle.

I guess in hindsight I should have known Maine was where I'd remain. I didn't really want to live in a huge metropolis anymore, with an exhausting—though exciting—semi-glam lifestyle and all the demands required to pay for it. I have always preferred quiet lakes, forests of towering trees and two-lane back roads to mega-tall skyscrapers, an energetic bar scene and harrowing commutes on jam-packed freeways. As much as I loved my life in Los Angeles, this place of mountains and harbors, anglers and boatbuilders, artists and outdoors enthusiasts was where I belonged.

That was the beginning. I spent a few years working odd jobs, winding my way from the MidCoast about ninety miles southwest into Maine's Lakes and Mountains Region. There I snagged a blogging gig for Maine's largest daily newspaper, the *Portland Press Herald*, writing about food and agriculture. Over the next couple years, assignments took me all over the state from potato farms in the northernmost part of Maine to small mill towns that no longer had working mills in the heart of the state's logging industry. I met all sorts of people and often was fascinated by their stories and grateful for their hospitality.

Along the way I started hiking—primarily in Acadia National Park, but gradually almost exclusively in the White Mountains of New Hampshire and in western Maine. During early morning drives to trailheads, I got to see a lot of the state that has inspired Stephen King. As a longtime reader of his work, I could envision a secluded wooded area on the edge of town with the remains of old cars rusting away as something he would chew on. A town without a stoplight, but a huge mausoleum? That seems just weird enough for King.

Inspired by these places I was seeing, I began rereading King's work that is set in Maine. As I read, I began recording in a notebook where stories were set. Sometimes, while reading, I'd stop and pull up his biography or Google his name and a location. I was fascinated to learn how much time he spent in these towns I was randomly visiting for work or passing through on my way to go for a hike.

I'm a curious person who loves maps, patterns, stories and a challenge. So, of course, I fell headlong into his Castle Rock universe. Hours were spent sitting cross-legged reading and rereading many of King's Maine-based stories. As I did this, I began noticing patterns. His characters overwhelmingly enjoy greasy hamburgers and apple pie à la mode. For a while, they drank Coke, then switched to Pepsi and eventually went back to Coke. Methodist churches linger throughout his fictional valleys, as do railroad tracks and the haunting ruins of industrial complexes. Birds stalk the skies.

King has an indisputably intimate knowledge of the places he writes about and bases his fictional universe on. His own real-life experiences and people he has known provide inspiration for scenes and characters. King notices the details in daily life that capture a sense of place and make his stories come alive. He walks you down main streets into popular cafés with candy-red leather stools and sticky counters for a cup of watered-down coffee. He checks you into a motel by abandoned tracks where the beds are made once a week and the air conditioner blows hot air.

I knew the towns of Castle Rock and Jerusalem's Lot, like a few other towns in the vicinity where his stories take place, do not really exist. However, looking at maps of Maine, I could see he imagined them somewhere just east of the New Hampshire–Maine border, west of Augusta and right around Lewiston and Bridgton.

In 2020, I produced an online story called "Stephen King's Maine," where I assembled maps of Castle Rock and Jerusalem's Lot, along with real-life locations that inspired him and where he set stories. At the time of publication in the spring of 2024, over twenty-eight thousand people have checked the story out.

In the fall of 2022, my friend Michelle Souliere, the proprietor of my favorite Portland literary haunt—the Green Hand Bookshop—asked me if I'd thought about adapting my online story on King's Maine into a book. Another writer friend, Monica, had suggested I update the story and include itineraries for weekend getaways. I trust both these women implicitly, and always longing for any reason to get out on the road and talk to strangers about their lives, I said yes! In short order, Michelle introduced me to her publisher, I spent a few days mapping out the story I wanted to tell and you now hold in your hands the result.

THE BOOK'S SECTIONS ARE organized geographically. Each one provides context regarding how the place has influenced King. As you wind your way through Portland, Lisbon Falls, Orono and other towns, you'll be introduced to the people who know this land the best, people who have made their home there—a gravedigger, police officer, librarian and more. Some are individuals whose lives have intersected with King because of where they live and what they do for a living.

The second section, "Coming of Age," presents a picture of Durham, Maine—where King spent the bulk of his adolescent years. With Doug Hall—a childhood neighbor of King's—in the driver's seat, we'll embark on a tour of Durham, beginning with the church that inspired a villainous house in King's novel *Salem's Lot*.

In "Interlude: Castle County, Castle Rock," we'll explore some of the exact locations found in King's fictional world of Castle County and learn about the businesses that conceivably inspired the main street mainstays of not just Castle Rock but also his other fictional towns, including Chamberlain and Jerusalem's Lot. For this chapter, I sought out old-timers in Lisbon Falls to learn about what Main Street looked like when King was there between 1958 and 1966. Some locals, like Ron Huston and Bryce Hamilton, had almost total recall when talking about the Lisbon Falls of their childhood.

Many of the mostly out-of-the-way places included in this book are anchored by those classic small towns where residents keep an eye out for one another and carry a quiet pride of their hometown. Some towns have shaken off their economic woes and found ways to develop or even flourish. Others are shells of their old selves. All, like I would imagine small towns everywhere, have a Norman Rockwellian–like idyllic surface—equal parts Twin Peaks (surreal and dark) and Mayberry (quaint and simple).

AT THE END OF the book is a sort of choose-your-own-adventure section with a couple of self-guided three-day itineraries should you—upon reading this book—feel an overwhelming desire to explore Maine. Book lovers, I've made sure you get your literary fix with literary landmarks and listings for my favorite independent bookstores.

1

NOTABLE AMERICAN
ORIGINS: PORTLAND

Just after Stephen King was born on Sunday, September 21, 1947, a fiendish group of grotesque undersea creatures devoured the state's lobster fleet, and a flock of gulls attacked a bus full of cannery workers. OK, no, not really. Actually, things would not get nightmarish until mid-October, when fires throughout Maine burned over 220,000 acres. It was the largest forest fire disaster in the state's modern history.

It turns out 1947 was the year pilot Kenneth A. Arnold saw a flying saucer while flying past Mount Rainier in Washington and Mack Brazel, a rancher outside Roswell, New Mexico, discovered unidentifiable debris people to this day believe are the remains of an extraterrestrial craft.

It was in the Maine General Hospital—now known as Maine Medical Center—at 22 Bramhall Street in Portland's West End, an enormous Victorian-era red brick structure with an imposing tower, that King was born.

The Portland into which King arrived was a city of around seventy-seven thousand, an old seaport with a waterfront lined with large sardine cannery warehouses. Downtown was filled with lobstermen, swordfish harvesters, long-liners, bait sellers and fish processors.

Munjoy Hill was still crowded with first-generation Italian families and mom-and-pop groceries. Clotheslines might have been strung between the three-story apartment buildings clustered together. At the Amato's on India and Newbury Streets, you could get a sandwich just as you can now.

Congress Street was bustling with clothing and footwear stores, and pig farms were situated where the Maine Mall now stands. The first section of the Maine Turnpike (I-95) was open only between Portland and Kittery.

King Connection

King never lived in Portland, but he visited occasionally to buy discounted comics while in high school. According to his childhood neighbor Doug Hall, the now defunct Porteous, Mitchell and Braun department store sold comic books with the covers torn off, so instead of a dime, you could get them for four cents. The stunning five-story 1904 Beaux-Arts building at 522 Congress Street is where the Maine College of Art is currently located.

King primarily uses Portland as a waypoint. In his novel *Cujo*, characters catch a bus at the old Greyhound Bus Terminal that was located at High and Spring Streets. Characters fly in and out of Maine at the Portland Jetport (*Pet Sematary*, *The Dark Half* and *Revival*). A rock 'n' roll station provides characters with everything from baseball game broadcasts to weather forecasts (*Salem's Lot* and *The Girl Who Loved Tom Gordon*).

If a character just wants to get away for a little while, there are motels aplenty (*Salem's Lot* and *Cycle of the Werewolf*). Other places mentioned are Deering Oaks Park (*Cujo*), the Eastern Promenade (*Gerald's Game*), the State Theater and Portland Headlight ("Night Surf").

And say a creepy antiques dealer in a fictional town called Jerusalem's Lot has a couple dozen coffins coming into the state one night, the pickup point is sure to be a shack at the end of Custom House Wharf at the Portland docks. At least, that's the way King writes it in *Salem's Lot*.

―――

MICHELLE SOULIERE—BOOKSTORE OWNER

Green Hand Bookshop occupies the ground-floor corner of the Trelawny Building at the intersection of Congress and Avon Streets in Portland's downtown district. After years of dreaming of running a bookstore, Michelle Souliere opened her shop there in 2009. It is apropos she chose this site, as until the 1950s the building was occupied by female

Michelle Souliere, owner
of Green Hand Bookshop
in Portland. *Photo by author.*

professionals—medical staff, a manicurist, a musical teacher, a dressmaker and a psychic, among others.

The shop is the go-to bookstore in Maine for science fiction anthologies, weird nonfiction (ghosts, UFOs, cryptozoology, occult) and long out-of-print mysteries—including those from Avon and Dell—the kind King devoured as a kid.

Michelle was born in 1973 and from kindergarten on grew up in Portland. She authored *Strange Maine: True Tales from the Pine Tree State* and *Bigfoot in Maine*. She is also the author and editor of the award-winning *Strange Maine* blog.

I wanted to speak with Michelle because her shop carries the most extensive stock of King's work I've seen in Maine and because King has a lifelong love of bookstores.

Michelle has always loved books. She grew up in a home with many of them and made regular visits to the Riverton branch of the Public Library.

Going Her Own Way in Portland

Michelle left home when she was sixteen and a junior in high school. She signed a lease on an apartment and lied about her age. She says no one even asked her for identification. Michelle explains Portland was smaller, and more fell through the cracks back then. The apartment Michelle rented for $260 a month was next to a convenience store and laundromat. The former is now a boutique hotel and spa and the latter my favorite café, Tandem Coffee and Bakery at 742 Congress Street.

She kept going to high school and working. Two weeks before she moved out, she informed her parents she would be leaving. Michelle told her mother she could call the cops, but that when they found out she was still in school and had a job and a place to live, because they were not rich, the police were not going to do anything about it. Michelle shares that her mom was really pissed because she found out this was true when she phoned the police.

Lovecraft 101

When Michelle was sixteen, her boyfriend at the time introduced her to writer H.P. Lovecraft's work, and she says it set her off on a whole realm of thinking. Lovecraft, a turn-of-the-twentieth-century author who lived in Providence, Rhode Island, is renowned for his weird fiction and horror. King is well-known as a fan of his writing.

> *What Lovecraft is able to do and King by succession is also able to do is to take the parts of Maine that if you're stuck in it probably seem oppressive and distasteful and create something that elevates it and gives it a characteristic that pushes it out of the ordinary. It is no longer mundane. It has surpassed mundane. It has achieved in some cases a bizarrely sublime existence.*

Michelle is attracted to Lovecraft's stories because they are relatable on a supernatural level. Anyone can have secrets; you don't have to be part of a rich old family that has generational secrets. Any tiny community can have secrets that the outside world doesn't know about and that are invisible most of the time.

In the mid-nineties, Michelle and her ski bum ex-boyfriend spent time at Maine's ski resorts, all of which are located near small towns hours from the coast.

It was winter so you saw everything at its dingiest and most barren. At some point, I had this epiphany that this was Lovecraft country. Especially when the sun is coming down. You're coming back from the mountain, you're exhausted, driving through all these tiny towns with homes with junked vehicles in their yards. Half tarped houses. Bare trees with none of the prettiness of the green leaves of summer or any of that going on. You catch a glimpse of the New England that Lovecraft writes about. I think that Lovecraft captured something in a way that nobody else had.

Michelle says she started thinking of January and February as Lovecraft season, and she would reread Lovecraft then because it seemed so suited to that time of the year. During the short dark days of winter, she finds places like Bridgton, a small lakeside town in western Maine, strikingly familiar to landscapes one can find in Lovecraft's work. "As the sun is going down, the snow-covered ground lacking signs of life, the bare trees and frozen lake evoke something ordinary, but otherworldly," she shares.

Opening a Bookshop

After selling books here and there for years while holding a full-time job and going to school, Michelle began reading about what is involved in bookselling. Her thinking was maybe, someday. Then in 2008, there was the financial crisis. She lost her job due to budget cuts, and her husband encouraged her—if not then, then when?

I had read Rebel Bookseller *by Andrew Laties, and at some point in the book he says to readers, "So you're thinking of opening a bookstore. Are you crazy?" Yep. I figured if I didn't try starting my own bookshop at that point in time, it would probably never happen. So, what the heck?*

Ever since, her days have been spent finding books for customers, answering emails, pricing books, cleaning books, packing books to mail away, organizing author events, getting bookcases installed and promoting new acquisitions and releases.

Hidden gems you might find in her shop at any given time include old pulp fiction, long-out-of-print mysteries, books on obscure topics from even more obscure authors, old sheet music, cookbooks and well-loved childhood favorites.

Portland has a long been a book haven, with multiple independent booksellers. It is a town of bibliophiles and inquiring minds.

JOEL BARNES—FOOT PATROL

In 1973, Joel Barnes began a twenty-five-year career with the Portland Police Department. During the seventies and eighties, Portland was gritty with a capital *G*. There were prostitutes working the downtown corners and nary a tourist in sight.

I wanted to speak with members of law enforcement, because two of King's most iconic characters are Sheriff George Bannerman (*The Dead Zone*, *Cujo*) and Sheriff Alan Pangborn (*The Dark Half*, *Needful Things*), each of whom presided over his fictional town of Castle Rock.

Coming of Age

Joel was born in 1948 in Portland and grew up near Deering Oaks Park.

> *People were there all summer. I'd get up in the morning and go out and not come in till the sun went down. You could walk anywhere. The Old Port was nothing but warehouses and the waterfront was fishing boat after fishing boat. If you go down to New Bedford, Massachusetts, and look at all those fishing boats, I think they all used to be in Portland Harbor. It was that busy. As time progressed and I grew you couldn't go into Deering Oaks anymore, especially if it was getting dark.*

Growing up, he was a little on the rowdy side: "I think what really changed my life was going into the military," he says. "I graduated from high school in 1966. I knew that everybody was getting drafted if they didn't have a deferment for school. I spent most of my high school years just drinking and raising hell. I really could not have gotten into college if my father was a millionaire."

Joel managed to get into the U.S. Air Force and feels he did pretty well by getting assigned to an aircraft control and warning squadron. He explains they controlled fighters and identified aircraft to make sure they weren't enemy aircraft. If they were, they'd scramble fighters after them.

Fresh out of high school in 1966, Joel landed at Keesler Air Force Base in Biloxi, Mississippi, for technical training. That was two years after the Civil

Rights Act. Yet in downtown Biloxi the water fountains and bathrooms, he recalls, still had signs designating them for "Whites" or "Colored."

"I'm with a couple of guys and one of them is Black and we wanted to go into a bar and get a beer and the Black guy says, 'I cannot go in there,'" Joel shares. "'They won't let me in there.' You never experienced that stuff up here." In 1969, he was stationed in Petersburg, Virginia, where he also witnessed racial segregation.

Those experiences are what defined him as a person.

Becoming a Police Officer

Starting out, Joel says you had to constantly be aware of your surroundings. You had to have street smarts, because—as he puts it—these people out there would eat you up in a minute.

"On my gun belt I had my holster, a handcuff pouch, little thing to hoop around my belt with a ring for my nightstick, and pouch that held about eighteen bullets," he shares. "That was it. Most guys would carry a buck knife or something in case you had to cut someone out of a car. Or if you come across someone who has been tied up. You don't want to untie that knot. You cut the rope."

The reason he says you cut the rope is because at that time DNA fingerprinting was not available. You wanted to see what kind of knot the person used. Certain kinds of knots might indicate the kind of job the person had—for example, if they were a sailor.

"Or if someone was tied up with duct tape," he adds. "You want to cut it because you don't want to damage the end of the duct tape, because it can tell you a lot of stuff. You can match a roll of duct tape. It's a piece. If you've got a circumstantial case, then you might need fifty or sixty pieces to put that case together."

The Blue Knight

Joel and his partner handled two housing projects and stayed busy with radio calls. On the 11:00 p.m. to 7:00 a.m. shift, they would check out businesses. "We would pull doors," he shares. "We knew places that had a habit of not locking their doors. That's why you had a beat. You'd drive by the back of a building and knew if it was a new or old pry mark. You'd know everything. If there was snow and there were fresh tire tracks. We even had sergeants that would leave a note on the door in the middle of the night, and it would say 'when you find this note call me.' Then if you didn't call them, they'd say well, why didn't you call me, didn't you find the note—you weren't checking the beat."

One of his favorite jobs was when he had a foot beat between 6:00 p.m. and 2:00 a.m. He walked both sides of Congress Street from Longfellow Square to Monument Square and then down to Cumberland Avenue and Spring Street. "You'd walk the beat and you'd get to know all these characters, and you'd break up a lot of fights," he says. "You'd catch tons of burglars. I can't tell you the number of times at one o'clock in the morning I'd be standing behind a building and hear a *tap tap tap* and then you call the owner and you get down there and you find somebody trying to pry the safe or something. All that stuff, and then you could go underground on Congress Street and go for blocks."

Prior to talking with Joel, I was only vaguely aware of the underground elements of Portland, thinking of them as mostly urban legends. No, he explains, they were very real. You could go down under the Westin, formerly the Eastland Hotel, and from the basement could walk all the way down to Cumberland Avenue—before the town built a parking garage—and all the way under those buildings and come up on Congress Street on Forest Avenue. On the corner of High and Congress Streets was a large Dunkin Donuts, and right next to it was an underground pool hall.

You can't be afraid. That's not a true statement. You can be afraid, you can feel a little bit of fright, or anxiety, but you had to do it. You committed yourself to a job. Like if you showed up and there was a fight call and you got there first, you couldn't stand around and wait. You had to deal with it. Maybe the military taught me that.

Joel is currently in the Cumberland County Sheriff's Office of Internal Affairs with plans to retire soon.

CHRISTOPHER PETERSON—CEMETERY SUPERVISOR

When people find out what Christopher Peterson does, the questions start flying. Have you seen dead bodies? What do you use to dig the graves? Have you been in the old tombs? Do the caskets really look like in the Western movies? The answers are: Yes. A backhoe. Yes. No.

Christopher was born in South Portland in 1984 and now lives in Westbrook. He supervises Evergreen Cemetery in Portland and Forest City Cemetery in South Portland. Between the two cemeteries, over eighty thousand people are interred.

For our interview, we meet up at Evergreen in the Deering Center neighborhood, where the thousands of monuments, duck ponds and network of paved and gravel trails attract locals and visitors alike. Of notable interest is the nineteenth-century Gothic-style Wilde Memorial Chapel, the memorial to former Portland mayor James Baxter and the Roman temple–like mausoleum where paper magnate Hugh J. Chisholm is buried.

Christopher has been working for Portland Cemeteries for sixteen years, rising from seasonal worker to supervisor. I wanted to speak with him because King has supporting characters who are gravediggers in his novels *Salem's Lot* and *The Dark Half*.

South Portland Childhood

Christopher says the South Portland of his childhood was a small, respectful place. He tells me his family molded him into who he is today. Christopher's father owned a mechanic shop. Before going to work in a cemetery, he figured being a mechanic or building houses was going to be his life.

"If someone told me this is what I'd be doing in high school I wouldn't have believed it," Christopher shares. "I'm glad I got all the experience, because we use it here—mechanics on the mowers and equipment. Helping to take care of the tombs, crypts and everything."

Grave Crew

He was hired on as a full-time mower and slowly worked his way up, becoming the third member of the grave crew. "It was a little weird for me at first," he says. "Death and stuff like that has never really bothered me

Christopher Peterson, cemetery supervisor. Photographed in Evergreen Cemetery in Portland. *Photo by author.*

per se. And at the time it was better to be on the grave crew to get a break from mowing."

Christopher shares that some of the grave crew had been digging graves for over three decades. Some had dug by hand before larger cemeteries switched to using backhoes in the 1970s.

Evergreen is more clay. "It's like putting a shovel in concrete," he explains. "It's really hard when it dries up, a lot more labor intensive. Your body is hurting by the end of the day." Forest City is all sand, which Christopher says is easier to dig, but you get a lot more cave-ins. During the winter, his crew has to use jackhammers at Forest City.

He walks me through the preparation for a gravesite once the grave is dug. "We put the fake greens down," Christopher says. "It's all boarded up underneath for support. The (lined and sealed) concrete box—the vault—is in the ground, and the greens drape around it so it looks nice and clean. Then we put the lowering device on top. That drops the casket down into the box. Then we pull the straps out and put the concrete cover on."

Hundreds of Acres of Concrete Boxes in the Ground

Disinterments—when someone is removed from a grave—are more common than people would think, Christopher tells me. He says he does one or two a year and that there are many reasons for them. He has even disinterred people in a cemetery and put them right back in the same cemetery in a different spot.

Very rarely, something unfortunate happens with a disinterment. "We were trying to do a disinterment over at Forest City," he shares. "This lady believed her cousin was over there and wanted to disinter her and bring her back to Africa, where the rest of the family was. When we started digging, we didn't know what we were going to find."

He found what he calls a four-piece box. For a period leading up to the early twentieth century, that is what people were buried in. The box consisted of a bottom piece that would be laid down and then four pieces would stand up around it with dirt up against them. That would be covered with two pieces.

"The person we were looking for was buried in the late 1800s/early 1900s," he explains. "Unfortunately, it definitely was not the person. It was a male, and we were looking for a female. He had a suit on, like a tuxedo. Still had hair, shoes on. Preserved because of the vault."

Christopher says that disinterment was one he did not want to do. He didn't feel he had enough information on the woman who was buried. He found a marker, the lot number and position, but he explains he has done a few of those—especially at Forest City—where things weren't documented back in the 1800s and early 1900s. "It could have been they were going to dig in one spot," he shares. "For some reason the next day they decided to be on another end of the cemetery and no one went back and corrected the information."

Digging a Grave

You're unlikely to see Christopher or his crew digging a grave. "We're pretty stealth about it," he says. "We're in and out. A lot of people who see it go the other way. Usually, it's just a truck and an excavator. We get it done fairly quick, cover it up and get out of there."

On the occasion when someone does see a grave being dug, they'll ask Christopher the following: "'How deep is the hole going to go?' 'What's that concrete box thing that goes in there?' Lot of questions about that. A lot of people see grass so they ask how do you know the exact place where the hole is being dug? How do you get them so straight?"

A: Five and a half to six feet deep.
A: The vault.
A: A computerized system, maps and individual lot markers. Some markers are on corners or no longer visible. They are made of concrete, stainless steel or aluminum.
A: Experience and equipment.

Processing Death

I've tried explaining this to quite a few other people before. I don't shut it out. It's not that. Death is not a thing to me anymore. It's kind of like a mechanic's car never runs right; a carpenter's house is never done. I don't know what happens after death, but it doesn't bother me. It's one of those things with the job. I'm not saying I'm looking to die or anything like that, but when it happens it happens. You're out here with thousands and thousands of people who have already been through it. They have died; they have passed on to whatever may be after. It's just not a...you kind of come to terms with dealing with it. It's hard for me when people come up to me and they say they've lost a loved one. I can sympathize with them, but it's just something that happens in life now. The thoughts of it, they just go away.

His Own End

Christopher wants to be cremated and have his son decide what to do with the ashes. He says just so long as no one has to maintain the land where they're scattered, he's good.

———

JOHN TANGUAY—FUNERAL DIRECTOR

The one thing you can be sure of in this world is that you will die. When that happens, your loved ones will grieve, and then they will have to decide on burial or cremation—if burial, they'll need to select a casket, choose a cemetery and maybe a florist, pick funeral music, obtain permits and so on. John Tanguay's job as a funeral director at Jones, Rich & Barnes is to guide people through the uncomfortable process of planning a funeral.

The business of death is in his blood. In the 1980s, when John was growing up in Gorham, his father was the superintendent at Brooklawn Memorial Park Cemetery in Portland. One of his sisters is the manager there now, and another worked in the crematory.

John apprenticed at Hay & Peabody's Funeral Home in 1995. An almost iconic part of Portland, the business ran from 1925 until about 2005. Old-timers would tell John stories about Hay, who was known for serving families regardless of their financial situation. His saying, according to those guys who knew Hay, was, "Well, we didn't make a lot of money this week but we made a lot of friends."

It was a very busy funeral home. Everybody loved this guy—Lloyd Hay. He had several hundred funerals a year. He had ambulances, a boat, a plane.

The first story in King's collection *If It Bleeds* is "Mr. Harrigan's Phone." The story is about a young boy who reads to an elderly wealthy industrialist named John Harrigan. When Mr. Harrigan dies, it is Hay & Peabody's Funeral Home who handles his funeral arrangements. The home also takes care of Joe Newall, a wealthy man who owned three mills in fictional Gates Falls in the 1920s in King's short story "It Grows on You," from his collection *Nightmares and Dreamscapes*.

Growing Up in a Cemetery

Growing up, John loved to be with his father and welcomed the opportunity to go with him to Brooklawn. There he helped out the groundskeeping crew.

All summer I would spend my whole week at Brooklawn Memorial. It was pretty cool. I'd run the lawn mower, weed wacker, and do trimming—things of that nature. I loved equipment, anything with an engine on it. One summer they pushed for flower beds, and I literally plucked dead flowers and watered all summer. I made one dollar an hour starting at around ten years old.

John describes his dad as honest, hardworking and with not a lot of education. A good man, he stresses. His father had twelve siblings and learned how to work at a young age. "He went in the service and married my mother," John shares. "He'd say people might not remember the things that you had, or what you collected, but they would always remember what kind of person you were. What kind of impact you had. He helped out a lot of people. He took a lot of his own time to help neighbors and friends with anything that he could contribute to."

His father's take on cemetery work is something John carries with him. "It was this person we may be taking care of today is not our family member, but it's somebody's and it could be ours someday and he would want someone to treat his family the same way," John says.

John tells me that to this day he'll drive through the cemetery and feel his dad's presence. "My family has always been there," he explains. "It was always part of our lives."

Mortuary School

When you graduate from mortuary school in the United States, you receive an associate's degree in mortuary science. There are the core classes—English and mathematics. Then there is restorative art. That's cosmetics for someone who has been damaged from some sort of trauma, John explains. And Embalming 101 and 102. These are classes about anatomy and microbiology as they relate to embalming.

"Without question my favorite class was anatomy," John shares. "I just happened to be very good at it, at memorizing. I graduated near top of my class."

Waking Up in a Body Bag

In 1994, while John was in mortuary school in Albany, New York, the county's coroner pronounced a woman as deceased and she woke up in the morgue. "It was the first Code Red in Albany Medical Center," he tells me. "They needed a crash team to come down."

John also says the coroner was quoted in the newspaper as saying, "She was cold as ice and stiff as a board," and that's how he determined she had passed.

Articles from the time said paramedics and the coroner found no heartbeat, no pulse, no breath or other signs of life, and the coroner declared her officially dead. They zipped her into a body bag and took her to the morgue at the hospital, where corpses are kept at forty degrees, and about ninety minutes later, the chief morgue attendant went to wheel her out of the cooler when he noticed the bag rising and detected a faint breathing sound. He opened the bag and found the woman alive. She did eventually die.

———

2
COMING OF AGE
GATEWAY: DURHAM

Standing in his front yard on Runaround Pond Road in Durham, Maine, his little house behind him shaded by numerous trees, an eleven-year-old Stephen King would have seen a neighbor's field spread out before him. His world was bookended by a modest white Greek Revival–style Methodist church to his left and a very small gravel pit to his right.

After spending parts of summers in Durham during his preschool years, King relocated there permanently from Connecticut with his mother, Ruth—his parents separated when he was two—and older brother, David, in 1958. It was in this small farming town where he picked up ideas for stories he has held onto for decades.

The house Stephen inhabited was rented to the family by his aunt Ethelyn, Ruth's younger sister, and uncle Oren Flaws in exchange for Ruth taking care of her and Ethelyn's parents. Ethelyn, a schoolteacher, and Oren, a contractor, lived in a two-story four-bedroom red brick farmhouse that sat across the field from his home.

Back in the 1950s, many of the roads there were still dirt and could be impassible during mud season (when the snow melts into slush and the rains come). Talk to anyone over sixty, and they can probably tell you this story: if their mother was due in April, she packed a bag and went to a family member's house in a town where there were paved roads. No woman wanted to get caught in the mud having a baby in the family pickup.

Located in Androscoggin County northwest of Portland, the town of a little over four thousand people hasn't changed much from when King grew up there. The roads were mostly paved by the 1960s. There are a still a fair number of family farms, and residents are still commuting to work in the neighboring towns of Freeport, Brunswick and Lewiston-Auburn. However, drive through town and you'll see a lot of modest one-story homes with plenty of life left in them being torn down for larger, modern homes. These and housing developments that would have been unheard of twenty years ago are cropping up to meet the needs of the working-class families who cannot afford nearby Portland's near-impenetrable real estate market.

During the autumn months, the long fields turn gold, and in early morning when the sun floats just above a mist, the little town can seem simultaneously magical and haunting.

Finding Inspiration

King's time here inspired some of his bloodiest books. The sixteen-year-old anti-villain in his first novel, *Carrie*, is modeled after two girls he went to school with. King has said he merged them to create Carrie White, a shy high school girl abused by her mother and bullied by her classmates. During a painful experience, Carrie's telekinetic powers are awakened and things blow up from there.

The Body, in his collection *Different Seasons*, is drawn from moments during his Durham years when he was absorbed in self-discovery. With incredible clarity, he tells of family dramas and experiences running around with a group of neighborhood kids. It is the ultimate coming-of-age story.

"Gramma," in his collection *Skeleton Crew*, is one of his creepiest reads. It's about an eleven-year-old boy left behind by his single mother one afternoon to care for his blind grandmother. In real life, King's grandmother was blind and bed-bound. One way to process his fear, assuming there was some, would certainly have been to write about it, even if years later.

His grasp of Durham and neighboring Lisbon Falls is personal, straightforward and perceptive. He tells it very much the way he lived it, with those glorious fictional tentacles taking root and dragging everything seemingly normal off like a urine-soaked sheet to expose something evil. All his fears, frustrations, joys and boyhood adventures are invested in the stories he sets in fictionalized versions of these towns.

It was 1959 or 1960 in the attic above the garage of Oren and Ethelyn's home where King's literary journey got a jump-start. He wasn't looking for treasure in an old footlocker, but that's what he found in the form of paperbacks once owned by his father. I imagine him sitting down, his back leaning against the cold metal trunk, his hands slightly sweaty, carefully turning the pages of H.P. Lovecraft's *The Lurking Fear and Other Stories*. The collection of twelve stories is the essence of weird fiction, of wholesome landscapes that become something terrible after dark, where strange events happen.

King was inspired by Lovecraft's ability to take actual places in New England and transform them into strange and ruined worlds. King's childhood years in Durham and Lisbon Falls are the inspiration for several of his fictional towns: Chamberlain, Jerusalem's Lot, Castle Rock, Gates Falls and Harlow.

In his novel *IT*, his preteen years in Durham are given a nod. He has said the fictional Maine town of Derry, where the story is set, is based on Bangor, Maine. However, two aspects of the book stand out as being drawn from King's real life in Durham. King arrived there in 1958, and the book largely takes place during the summer of 1958. Also, the group of bruised adolescents who battle a dancing monster clown by the name of Pennywise could embody the group of neighborhood kids he ran around with in Durham, kids he was going to horror movies with—just like the kids in the book.

———

DOUG HALL—LOCAL KNOWLEDGE, BOYHOOD FRIEND

Doug Hall, born in 1942, grew up in the part of Durham known as Methodist Corner. He hung out with King's older brother, David, and cousin Donald Flaws.

Doug has helped me to piece together what King's childhood experience looked like in Durham and neighboring Lisbon Falls. King was a walker even as a child but never cut through fields. He always walked around them. It was the Hall house where the neighborhood kids went for the chocolate chip cookies his mom made because she thought the kids were too skinny. There King read the DC Comic featuring the World War II soldier Sergeant Franklin John Rock.

Methodist Corner is named for its proximity to the West Durham Methodist Church near the intersection of Runaround Pond, Hallowell and Rabbit Roads.

Doug says that when the King boys arrived, they were received into a ready-made social network offering local history, introductions and information about the town and neighboring towns.

> *In Methodist Corner, we hung with a small pack of children who all lived a house apart till we reached high school age and then largely splintered with contact limited to weekends and summers. Kids went to Freeport, Brunswick, Lisbon, Auburn and Yarmouth for high school. At dances we tried to impress our peers by bringing dates from other schools.*

The Area Kids as Described by Doug

HALL BOYS: Doug (Douglas as a child); his younger brother Brian, who was Stephen's age and one of his closest friends; Dean; and Dana. They enjoyed comics, horror movies, poker and blackjack and did not read many books. Doug went to Lisbon Falls High School.

CHESLEY BOYS: The five boys didn't go to church or high school with the Hall brothers or King.

BROWN GIRLS: The three girls went to high school in Freeport. One, whom Doug describes as creative, might have been the most involved in church, Thursday night youth group and ice skating. They went to the Marston place—the abandoned house served as inspiration for King's fictional Marsten House in the novel *Salem's Lot*.

DONALD FLAWS, Stephen's cousin, lived in what the kids called the "brick house" and went to high school in Brunswick, just like David King did.

Local News

Doug's mother wrote a weekly column for the *Lisbon Enterprise* about goings-on in Methodist Corner—covering everything from a baby shower to when King's grandfather Guy Pillsbury went to the hospital. "I think she made ten cents an inch," Doug says.

David published a newsletter called *Dave's Rag* about what was going on in Methodist Corner. Stephen contributed stories. According to Doug, everybody in the neighborhood read it. Myrtle Harrington, a West Durham neighbor, gave David an old typewriter the *n* tab didn't work on. Doug says David would write in every *n* with a pencil. As a thank-you, Stephen named a street after her in his fictional town of Castle Rock.

Bookmobile

Around 1953, the Maine State Library began bookmobile service to Durham and other rural areas without a library.

A bookmobile would come by, and you could pick out books. It was smaller than a FedEx truck but shaped like one, and I believe it was green. You could go in, or at least, little kids could. Maybe the side opened up. I read relatively simple books like The Lone Ranger. *Steve probably read more books in a month than I did in a year. He was just way beyond.*

In a 2006 interview with the *Paris Review*, King talks about picking out Ed McBain's 87th Precinct novels. The books, about a detective squad in New York City in the 1950s and 1960s, King says marked the end of his reading juvenile fiction. He was attracted to the realness and grittiness.

Not a Converted Hearse

Doug says the rumors that King rode to school in a converted hearse are just that. He explains it was his brother Brian, with whom King was good friends, who eventually had the converted hearse.

Mike Yenco, whom Doug describes as a big, gruff, cigar-smoking guy, was who parents paid one dollar a week to drive their child to school in Lisbon Falls.

He kept getting bigger cars. Cars with two rows, then three rows. Eventually he got a Cadillac, that might resemble a hearse. You could officially sit four or five kids in it. He, at times, may have snuck in an extra kid. When getting near the (Lisbon) Falls bringing all these kids, he'd occasionally pick up a girl from a trailer and there would not be enough room in the cab for her, so Stephen being the biggest, she got to sit on his lap for the last mile. I think she's a piece of Carrie (the titular character of his novel Carrie*) but who knows.*

TOUR OF DURHAM

Doug invites me on a tour of Durham, starting at Shiloh Church and retracing part of Mike Yenco's route, with him and his wife, Dorris. He relates that getting from point A to point B was one of the major challenges in King's youth. For reference, I've included a map on pages 50–51 of the route through West Durham into Lisbon Falls.

Shiloh Chapel
38 Beulah Lane

The Shiloh Temple, now Shiloh Chapel, is a facility associated with a religious organization known as the Kingdom.

If you don't live in Androscoggin County, Maine, you have likely never heard of Frank Sandford, so let me enlighten you. He was born in Bowdoinham, Maine, in 1862. As a boy, he played baseball and worked on the family's farm. After attending a religious recruitment meeting at the age of eighteen, he became a fundamentalist Baptist and eventually a pastor.

In 1893, he arrived literally and figuratively in Durham. A Maine-based Christian youth society welcomed him and encouraged his proselytizing. A local businessman by the name of Douglas Sandhill donated a vacant farmhouse on a treeless hill just off River Road.

Within a few years, Sandford was well on his way to creating an evangelical empire. Word of his renowned sermons had spread. Demanding not only unfailing loyalty but also all of his followers' earthly possessions and their labor, he set about building a home for his growing congregation. In 1897, the white structure with a seven-story high tower topped with a gold-colored dome known as "Jerusalem's Tower" was completed atop the hill.

Fast-forward to 1911: after years of traveling the globe as a missionary, Sandford sailed into Portland Harbor with a rundown boat and crew members who had died of scurvy. He was arrested and convicted of manslaughter. The religious movement he had built, by then known as the Kingdom, continued during the decade he spent in federal prison. Sandford died penniless.

In King's sophomore novel *Salem's Lot*, the Marsten House is a house on a hill overlooking the fictional town of Jerusalem's Lot. King writes it as something evil, almost alive and watchful. Shiloh Church is believed by many, including myself, to be the physical inspiration for the Marsten House.

"THEY'D WHISPER THE SHILOHITES"

We depart Shiloh, turning right onto Shiloh Road and then left onto Pinkham Brook Road (Route 125), a relatively quiet two-land road save for the dump trucks traveling dangerously fast.

As we drive by beige fields, Doug recounts how the church bought up much of the farmland around it, frightening the town. "Farmers had had full control," he says.

> *Suddenly there were six hundred new people in our schools and the church was buying all the farms in town. That was traumatic for the town and that lasted for decades. When I was growing up, they'd whisper the Shilohites. Steve would have been aware of them, because they went to high school with us. The girls didn't wear make-up, had their hair in a bun and wore long dresses similar to Mennonites.*

King references the Shiloh Church in his novel *Revival*, placing it in his fictional town of Harlow. The young protagonist in the story references his dad considering them "serious weirdos."

Shiloh Chapel in West Durham, built between 1896 and 1897. *Photo by author.*

Rabbit Road

After a couple minutes, we turn right onto Quaker Meeting House Road, which ultimately crosses Royalsborough Road (Road 136), where it turns into Rabbit Road.

On Rabbit Road, I see no rabbits. However, Doug points out a spot where there used to be a little camp with a hired hand who had a hook and a small pond where the kids used to skate. This road is where King's Durham world really began. The Brown family lived here, and next to their home was an old Cape-style house owned by the Marston family.

Marston House

The idea of the previously mentioned fictional Marsten House in King's novel *Salem's Lot* is thought to have originated from an old Cape on Rabbit Road. The real-life Marston family moved to Durham from Scarborough and, according to Doug, ran a big farming operation. Bertha Marston (formerly Harmon) married Lewis Marston, and they moved into the house on Rabbit Road. Why it was abandoned in the early 1960s is unknown. According to their headstones in Cedar Grove Cemetery in Durham, Lewis died in 1951 and Bertha in 1975.

All that remains is a rock foundation, but according to Doug, the house was there in 1965. "We used to crawl in through the back window," he says. "The table was set for the next meal even though no one was living there."

Doug was not involved with making a movie in the house but believes King may have been. "I think I heard about it and vaguely recall his brother (David) borrowing a camera and they made some movies," he tells me.

The Parsonage

On the other side of the Brown family home, close to where Rabbit Road intersects with Hallowell Road (Route 9), Doug indicates a sweet-looking house on the right that was formerly the parsonage. This was where the church's Thursday night Methodist Youth Fellowship meetings were held in the 1950s and 1960s. The King brothers regularly attended, singing hymns and reading Bible verses. Doug says King's aunt Ethelyn Flaws sometimes assisted with teaching the younger kids.

Foundation of the Marston family home in West Durham. Inspired location in the novel *Salem's Lot*. Photo by author.

King is a big fan of Charles F. Huff, the lay preacher who was also the Orr's Island postmaster. In his 1984 speech "Huffy," he describes Huff as a man with a contagious sense of humor who provided wildflowers for the church, organized field trips for the kids to Bradbury Mountain in Pownal and Thomas Point Beach in Brunswick, generously supplied the food for picnics and paid any park admission fees.

In *Revival*, King writes about a young likeable reverend who arrives in a small town and charms the Methodist Church's congregation and attendees of the Thursday Night School. The church is located on fictional Methodist Road near the real-life intersection of Route 9.

> *On Old Home Sunday when we celebrated the anniversary of the church, everyone was welcome to come in and eat. Stephen was sometimes a waiter, as we all were. People sat down to eat beans. When we'd run out of rolls on the table you ran to get some more.*

"The Last Rung on the Ladder"

The Halls used to own a large barn that in a previous lifetime had been a general store and post office on the southeast corner of Hallowell (Route 9) and Rabbit Roads.

"My father took the stairs out so we'd stop playing upstairs," Doug tells me. "He thought it was unsafe. I don't know if Steve ever played there, but it would have been a horror place. Creepy, like the Marston House." Doug says the kids would dare each other to climb to the high spot after his dad took the stairs out. He thinks this inspired King's story "The Last Rung on the Ladder" from his short story collection *Night Shift*.

In the book, the story is set in Omaha, Nebraska. This doesn't mean it wasn't based on childhood events in Durham. King not infrequently picks up real and fictional towns and moves them around to adjust for his storytelling.

Route 9

In King's universe, Route 9 travels from Portland to his fictional towns of Gates Falls and Castle Rock and into real-life Lewiston.

At Hallowell Road (Route 9), Rabbit Road turns into Runaround Pond Road. At the intersection, head east, and this is where Doug and his brothers lived. Travel west, and the brick house still stands where the Flaws, King's aunt and uncle, lived.

One-Room Schoolhouse

On the northeast corner of Route 9 and Runaround Pond Road there used to be a one-room schoolhouse where King attended sixth or seventh grade before a new (now defunct) school was built. The school had no running water and an outhouse out back. Water was carried down from the Halls' home and poured into a ceramic jug. The building was heated by a wood stove with wood stacked near the entryway for the boys to carry to the stove when needed. On average, a couple dozen kids attended at a time.

WEST DURHAM METHODIST CHURCH

After passing the school, we pull up by the tiny historic West Durham United Methodist Church (23 Runaround Pond Road). Charles F. Huff, the lay preacher, presided on Sundays. Here Ruth King played the piano and organ. Ethelyn Flaws substituted for her on occasion. Because Ruth was such a prodigious player, Doug says Ethelyn would say, "I'm sorry Ruth is not here today."

Doug shares a funny story about how his brother Brian scared King nearly to death one evening. "One night Brian and Steve were up late at our house watching horror movies," he says. "At midnight or so Steve trudged slowly down the hill and across the street toward his home (which was next to the church). Brian ran across the field and into the church. It wasn't locked in those days. As Stephen walked by, he came out the door screaming. Steve was terrified."

Methodist Church in West Durham, constructed in 1804. *Photo by author.*

Potential Cujo Farm

Cujo is King's novel about how a two-hundred-pound Saint Bernard goes from being a beloved pet to a rabies-stricken canine that terrorizes a small community. King has said the story came to him in 1977 when he went to get his motorcycle fixed outside the town of Bridgton and a huge dog came out of the garage growling at him. The mechanic stopped the dog from doing any harm, but King was unsettled enough to write what became one of his most famous novels about it.

As with many things related to King, throughout Maine, people lay claim to a story's origins. Sure enough, Doug points out a homestead on Runaround Pond Road he thinks could have partially inspired King's *Cujo*.

> *Bertha Harmon lived there with her sister until she married a Marston and moved into the house on Rabbit Road. We always called it the Collie farm. They had six to eight dogs that would run out in the road and attack cars. To go the Chesley's or the little general store for cigarettes, ice cream or sodas, Steve had to walk by this place. The dogs were running around and looked like they might bite you. It's one of a few farms that could have inspired where* Cujo *took place.*

Runaround Pond

In the prologue of King's novel *The Dead Zone*, six-year-old protagonist Johnny Smith is hit hard by an older much larger boy on the ice on Runaround Pond in Durham and passes out. He survives, but the accident goes on to haunt him years later.

In King's novella *The Body* from his collection *Different Seasons*, a group of twelve-year-old boys goes swimming and when cleaning themselves off realize they have leeches on them. Panic rightfully ensues, creating one of the most memorable parts of the story. According to Doug, there are a lot of leeches in the pond and it's more for wading than swimming. Sure enough, he says King got bloodsuckers on him at least once.

Runaround Pond in Durham. Inspired a scene in King's novella *The Body*. *Photo by author.*

ODD JOBS

After checking out the pond, we head back onto Runaround Pond Road the way we came. We then detour onto Davis Road, where we pass the old Chesley home and farther up to Harmony Grove Cemetery on the edge of some woods. With its low stone wall and black wrought-iron gate sitting just up from the crest of the hill, it looks just like the Harmony Hill Cemetery King describes in *Salem's Lot*, sans the vampire.

King knows Harmony Grove well. He and Brian Hall dug a grave for Ed Newell, an old man who passed away from natural causes who had lived in King's house before him. "Brian referred to him as Dead Ed," Doug says. "He and Steve would invent names. I dug Bertha Marston's grave. You dug your neighbors' graves. We used to get ten to fifteen dollars to dig a grave."

Doug says the first time he had to dig a grave he was pretty concerned about having to dig down six feet, because that's what always happened in the Western movies. He was relieved when he learned he only had to dig four feet down.

In front of the cemetery, Doug allays the rumor King ever spent the night in it. He is pretty sure that is an urban legend.

The kids in the neighborhood worked odd jobs for spending money, which they used to buy junk food at a local shop, discount comics and movie tickets. Digging graves, haying and harvesting potatoes were a few jobs.

> *After we'd hay there was this one pond where cows would go in the water. It smelled like cow poop, but haying out in the sun, it's hot, and you are sneezing, and itching. So, we'd jump into the cow pond. Steve swam down there. We'd get a buck a day for haying.*

Doug says he enjoys reading King's stories and trying to figure out who King is writing about, if it's someone they grew up with.

> *He'll blend two or three people into one....You're reading and you think you know who he's writing about and then he'll blindside you with not quite. Like he talks about picking rocks in the garden, and we used to pick rocks. First thing in the year before you harrow or right after you harrow so the planters and cultivators won't hit rocks. Every year the rocks come back and we'd ask where do these rocks come from. King would write about the farmer who was picking rocks and his hands are bleeding. Dried and cracked and my father's hand always looked like that. We used to joke about his bloody hands. So, Steve starts writing about the farmer with bloody hands, and you think he's writing about my father, but then he brings someone else in.*

In King's novel *IT*, one of the major protagonists of the story, Mike Hanlon, grew up on a farm. In June 1958, Hanlon recalls how every April and May the work would begin with what he calls a rock harvest. Every day for one week, he would pick up rocks as his father drove the tractor breaking up the soil and digging up weeds. He doesn't mention bloodied hands, but it's possible King includes rock harvesting in another story.

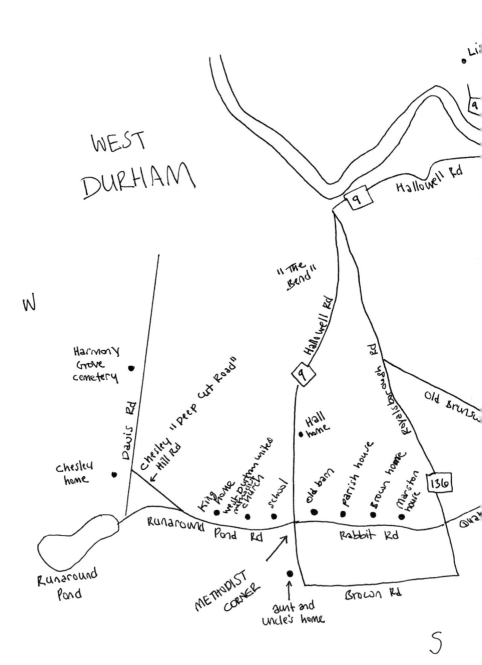

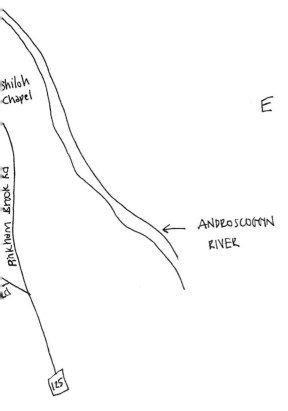

Hand-drawn map of West Durham neighborhood and Stephen King's route to Lisbon Falls High School. Informed by Doug Hall. *Illustration by author.*

DEEP CUT ROAD

We turn around and go back down Davis Road, making a left onto an unpaved road called Chesley Hill Road that runs between Davis Road and Runaround Pond Road. According to Doug, King calls this stretch "Deep Cut Road." King fans might be familiar with this road. King mentions it in *Salem's Lot* (the love interest Bonnie Sawyer lives on it), and in *Under the Dome* it runs between two fictional towns.

THE BEND

After picking up King and Brian Hall at the Halls' home, Mike Yenco would have traveled up Route 9 toward Lisbon Falls. On the way, he would have passed through an area King refers to as "the Bend." He places it in his town of Jerusalem's Lot in *Salem's Lot* and Castle Rock in his short story "It Grows on You" from his collection *Nightmares & Dreamscapes*. In both, it is a place where land is cheap and people live in mobile homes. In real life, there was a trailer there when King was going to high school. According to Doug, it is where one-half of the Carrie White character lived.

Practical Information Should You Decide to Replicate This Tour

START: Durham Get & Go (697 Royalsborough Road) or Shiloh Chapel (38 Beulah Lane), both in Durham
FINISH: Little River Coffee (11 Union Street) in Lisbon Falls
SUGGESTED TIME: Allow one hour so you can really take your time.

3
VISIONS

LISBON FALLS

It's standing-room-only in the Lisbon High School gymnasium at eight o'clock on an evening in early June 1966. Donning caps and gowns, around one hundred graduating seniors are moving on after four years of creating memories. Some are going on to work as secretaries, having mastered shorthand and typing in Miss Ellen Margitan's commercial classes. Others will seek work as plumbers or carpenters, and some young men will travel overseas to the Central Highlands of South Vietnam.

In this crowd is a young King, who made honor roll his freshman and sophomore years, edited the school newspaper *The Drum* his junior year and played a sadistic "wanted" criminal in the senior play *Arsenic and Old Lace*.

In King's novel *Carrie*, the prom at Thomas Ewen High School is a pivotal scene, the equivalent of the fairy tale ball from the Cinderella story gone wrong. The Spring Ball Decoration Committee has been decorating the gym for the main event, themed Springtime in Venice. George Chizmar is called out as the school's most artistic student. His mural of gondolas on a canal at sunset is described in detail.

In real life, John Chizmar was a talented artist and classmate of King's at Lisbon High School. For the school's 1965 homecoming coronation, themed Enchanted Castle, he created a mural of an old English castle. Of note, at the same event, King performed a folk duet with his friend Maureen Babicki.

Writing

During his high school years, King wrote a story called "Mousetrap," which takes place during predawn hours in a market, pitting a young man by the name of Kelly against a recently installed very much alive burglar device sporting an electric brain and limber-jointed steel tentacles. But that's not all—a display of canned soup and an expensive rump roast also play into the mix. There's blood of course, a lot of blood.

King stretched his writing muscle outside school as well, as a sportswriter for the *Lisbon Enterprise* under the tutelage of editor and writer John Gould. In his 2000 book *On Writing: A Memoir of the Craft*, King writes about how Gould taught him about writing for himself and writing for others.

Gould, in addition to editing the *Lisbon Enterprise*, wrote a weekly column for the *Christian Science Monitor* and in 1947 authored his best-known book, *The House That Jacob Built*, about rebuilding his great-grandfather Jacob's 1780 farmhouse in Lisbon Falls.

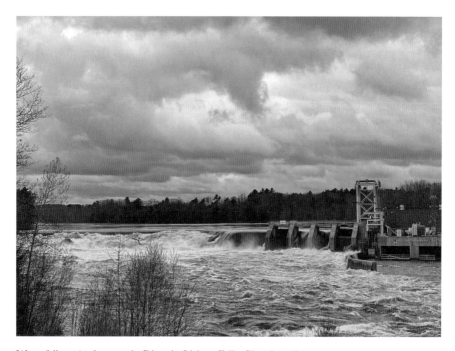

Waterfall on Androscoggin River in Lisbon Falls. *Photo by author.*

Lisbon and Lisbon Falls

Lisbon Falls is a village in the town of Lisbon. The actual border that separates Lisbon and Lisbon Falls—formerly known as Little River—is the Sabattus River, a tributary of the Androscoggin River. From the Sabattus west is Lisbon. Lisbon had a combined population of around 9,600 in 2020. In 1960, when King lived in the area, the population was closer to 5,000.

Lisbon Falls has been described to me by people who grew up in it in the fifties, sixties and seventies as being a very different version back then of what it is now. There were fewer strangers. You recognized everyone. Parents, siblings, even cousins of kids you went to school with. Everybody knew who was married to whom and who might be drinking a bit too much. When a young man who graduated from Lisbon High School in 1964 was killed in Vietnam in 1968, there was collective mourning.

People who grew up there stayed. When President Lyndon Johnson passed through the area in 1964, having landed nearby at the now decommissioned Brunswick Naval Air Station, Ron Huston remembers sitting with relatives on the steps of his great-grandparents' house watching the motorcade. Ron, who was born and raised in Lisbon Falls, recalls Jane Beganny, whom he describes as having been a popular kindergarten teacher in the fifties and sixties, as was her mother, Mabel Dearnley, before her for several decades.

The village, and really all of Lisbon, Huston tells me, was energized by the Worumbo Manufacturing Company's woolen mill. When it went, it took the lifeblood out of the town.

Industrial Past

Beginning in the latter part of the nineteenth century, until the mid-1960s, the lives of many of the town's residents pivoted around several manufacturing businesses. The best known were the Worumbo Mill established in 1864 at the end of Main Street on the bank of the Androscoggin, where the Worumbo Hydro Station currently sits, and a paper company incorporated in 1889 operating under different names—most memorably as the U.S. Gypsum Mill. It was located on Route 196 where a used car dealership is as you leave town heading toward Topsham.

Earlier sawmills were washed away in 1814, and in 1901 a fire destroyed thirty-one downtown buildings.

Intersection of Lisbon Street (Route 196), Canal Street (Route 9) and Main Street (Route 125). Looking at former Worumbo Mill site in downtown Lisbon Falls. *Photo by author.*

It was a fire, ignited when a worker's torch fell into combustible materials, on July 23, 1987, that destroyed the sprawling red brick structure that made up most of the Worumbo Mill. Older residents of Lisbon Falls watched as years of memories went up in flames rising high into the air.

The mill had survived into the 1970s under the name of the Lisbon Weaving Company, after nearly six hundred employees were laid off in July 1964 by Worumbo. The fire left only a shell of the original structure, which was demolished in 2016. The white building standing today was part of an expansion in the 1920s.

"We watched it burn," resident Maggie Barnard shares. "Standing by the library by where it was roped off. My mom was crying. The whole town was like that. When the mill burned down it was a moment for us that coincided with a lot of businesses that had been thriving before kind of aging out. It felt like the place was in a kind of limbo after that."

Rats

King spent the summer after high school graduation in 1966 working at the Worumbo Mill with Doug Hall's younger brother Brian. In *On Writing*, King details working an eight-hour shift at Worumbo, a place he describes as

Dickensian. Maybe it was, but King turned it into an opportunity. The natural storyteller in him took his dismal experiences there to fuel his imagination.

In 1970, *Cavalier*, a popular men's magazine between the 1950s and 1970s, paid King for a short story he based on something that happened at the mill. During the Fourth of July week, some of the guys he worked with cleaned the mill from top to bottom, including the basement. King recalls in *On Writing* how they told him they saw rats as big as dogs. The story, "Graveyard Shift," is also part of his collection *Night Shift*.

In the story, a mill worker with a fear of rats is recruited to help clean the basement level of the mill, which has not been touched in over a decade. It is rough work for a few days, and then it is the stuff of waking nightmares, which King is so good at producing. Lack of sunlight and years of neglect had given the mill's already plentiful rat population an unprecedented opportunity to boom and mutate. There in the subterranean darkness King takes the reader to the edge of an "all-you-could-eat buffet."

Doug Hall, who worked at the U.S. Gypsum Mill with his father for three summers, conveys to me with some disgust how scary the big river rats were. Other individuals I speak with confirmed seeing rat infestations in the basements of old mill buildings—especially when a river would run high.

Kennebec Fruit Company

For over ninety-nine years, the Kennebec Fruit Company sat at the corner of Main Street and Route 196 across the street from the site of the Worumbo Mill. In front of the two-story beige-colored building, Lamberto Anicetti began selling peaches, pears and apples in old-fashioned wooden crates during the warmer months. His son Frank came along in 1916, around the time he opened the store. In 1940, Frank Anicetti Jr. arrived and by his teenage years was helping out.

According to Doug, one wall of the store had bandages, cigarettes and other odd and ends people might need. In the winter, that section was skimmed down and the crates of fruit were put up against the wall.

There was also a marble-topped ice cream parlor inside, and Doug claims with some conviction they had the greatest ice cream floats. In the 1960s, when King was in high school, that end of Main Street would have been bustling with families and mill workers going on or coming off shift. The arrival of warm weather made the Kennebec Fruit Company a popular neighborhood spot.

Doug says Durham kids would stand on the corner outside the shop by the telephone pole and wait for a lift home. U.S. Gypsum, which ran three shifts 24/7, was where Doug's dad, an electrician, and his buddies worked. Depending on when one of them got off, they'd pick up Doug and his brothers and take them home or close to home. "It was an era when you knew everybody and everybody knew you. There was no fear of strangers," Doug tells me.

King would stand on that corner waiting for a ride and talking to Frank Anicetti Sr. and his son Frank "Mr. Moxie" Anicetti Jr., the latter of whom he immortalized in his 2001 time-traveling novel *11/22/63* about a Lisbon high school teacher who attempts to prevent the JFK assassination. The book was adapted into a miniseries that aired on Hulu in 2016, the same year Frank Anicetti Jr. retired.

In the book, the protagonist, Jake Epping, a recently divorced high school English teacher, travels back to Lisbon Falls in September 9, 1958, where he sees the Worumbo Mill—Dickensian as ever—and goes into the nearby Kennebec Fruit Company to indulge in a ten-cent root beer that's served to him by Frank Anicetti Sr. in a large frosty mug with foam on top. King describes the shop as selling fruit, comics and newspapers and having a marble-topped soda fountain.

In *Carrie*, which takes place in his fictional town of Chamberlain, Maine, King turns the Kennebec Fruit Company into the Kelly Fruit Company,

Vintage postcard depicting the Kennebec Fruit Company in Lisbon Falls in latter half of twentieth century. *Courtesy of the Lisbon Falls Historical Society.*

which is run by a less-than-likeable man by the name of Hubert Kelly. The shop is a combination grocery and soda fountain. It sells alcohol, pornography and cigarettes. One of the supporting characters, Sue Snell, orders "a dime root beer" that's served in a huge, frosted 1890s mug.

According to Ron Huston, back in the sixties, the Kennebec Fruit Company served Rochester Root Beer. That was the "big" thing—and the root beer floats were famous. He remembers walking by the store as a child and how it smelled of fruit.

Moxie

Frank Anicetti Jr. took over the store in the late seventies and continued doing what his father and grandfather had done before him. He continued to sell the orange-labeled "distinctly different" carbonated beverage Moxie. He also displayed the family's collection of orange-tinged Moxie memorabilia. In the early 1980s, he held a book signing for Frank Potter, the author of *The Moxie Mystique*. Several hundred Moxie fans flocked to the signing, and the rest, they say, is history

Within a few years, there was a parade, and then the one-day event became a three-day festival with a recipe contest, 5K road race and car show. The Moxie Festival is held on the second weekend in July in Lisbon.

In 2005, Moxie was designated as the official soft drink of the State of Maine.

The Kennebec building was bought and turned into Frank's Restaurant and Pub. The owners have an old sign from the Worumbo Mill hanging by the bar, and laminated counters display a wonderful collage of vintage photos and Moxie memorabilia.

———

MAGGIE AND KATE—COFFEE SHOP PEOPLE

Besides being a great location with far better than average coffee and pastries, Little River Coffee at 11 Union Street has personality in spades. It's one of those places where you always feel welcome, in large part thanks to sassy co-owner Maggie Barnard, who is a regular behind the counter. The tin ceilings, hardwood floors and airy sunlit space make for a wonderful refuge any day.

The turn-of-the-century building they are in has housed the *Lisbon Enterprise* (in the basement), a hardware store and a recreation center and supposedly was a place where train employees stayed back when the Maine Central Railroad was running.

When I approached Maggie about interviewing her and her partner Kate for this book, I tried as subtly as possible to acknowledge my impression that King had been inspired by Lisbon Falls when creating his fictional town of Castle Rock, Maine. Maggie didn't bat an eye. Her response was along the lines of well, of course Lisbon Falls is Castle Rock.

Opening a Coffee Shop

Maggie was born in Waldoboro and moved to Lisbon at the age of one. Kate has lived in Lisbon since 2006. Through various iterations of familyhood and then careers and shifts and different aspects they became best friends. They have five children each and met when their oldest were babies.

"My oldest is six months older than her oldest," Maggie says. "To the day, and her baby is born on my birthday," Kate responds.

Maggie and Kate have been drinking coffee together for seventeen years, during which time they had varying creative phases. The one that led them to opening a coffee shop was what Kate describes as their "bakery and coffee making phase," during which they learned to make lattes, truffles and bread. They had more conversations about opening a coffee shop, and then thankfully they did in October 2021.

Kate tells me the idea remained in the backdrop, more dream than reality, as she and Maggie questioned whether they could do it. "You say it in the same way you're like I'm going to travel the world when I retire," Kate shares. "It sounds wonderful, and you really would like to and if given the opportunity maybe you would."

On Lisbon Falls

What first attracted Kate to Lisbon is that the people there have a real sense of their own identity. "It wasn't necessarily my identity," she explains. "It wasn't something I connected with from my upbringing. They were completely who they were unapologetically, but generously."

Kate grew up in Orrington, Maine; her parents were from Massachusetts, and she says they were outsiders their entire lives. "When we migrated to Bucksport, Maine, we lived in that whole Bangor area with all those small towns that had their own identities and they were fairly exclusive," Kate shares. "But Lisbon was 'this is who we are and this is how we live.' Some people would describe it as a couple decades in the past, like Lisbon is still very much a football town. People really live the glory days of their high school. Like you might read about in a story twenty or thirty years ago."

But she says it is so much more than that. People in Lisbon have invited her to participate in what she considers a strong community. "You know if you move here, you will belong to this community and they are here for you," Kate shares. "Very honest, authentic people. No apologies."

"Zero apologies," Maggie agrees.

They explain that in Lisbon Falls you don't have to apologize for being who you are. "Here I am and you're welcome to know it," Kate says.

They describe Lisbon culture as being very intergenerational. The majority of people they know here lived there because their parents lived there and their grandparents lived there. And a lot of times even their great-grandparents lived there. "A lot of people know everybody, and they honor that," Kate shares. "That is part of who they are. There's a lot of local lore. You know families. It's amazing to me [that] in a time where everybody I knew growing up left town, including me and all my siblings, a lot of people choose to remain here. That's a testament to the community."

"There are different flavors to it," Kate continues. "Like, Moxie is a big deal, but Moxie is only a big deal because it is such a great emblem for what the people here are like. They're independent and kind of feisty. A little bit different than mainstream."

Sometimes it takes a few interactions to really get to know people and like them, Maggie says. She feels the only people unwelcome in Lisbon are those who are—as she puts it—uppity. The realness of people there is a primary reason she has stayed in Lisbon and is growing her family there. "What you want are people around you who are real, because then you can be real," Maggie shares.

Kate says the community's support of the café has been incredible. That includes people who have been getting their coffee at McDonald's their whole life and go out of their comfort zone to go to Little River.

Not Your Average Town

There is a sixth sense here, something different. I don't mean it in a creepy or horror way. But there is something magical. I don't know if it's being by the river, but there's a fabric beneath things here. Stephen King is a master at noticing things and making people come to life through their habits, not just through a description. The characters here are real. They're not characters; they are real people. There is something about the space and time interaction here I think is very conducive to story. There are those elements. You have the mill, the river, the multi-generations. You have speckled throughout history petty crimes and some unsolved things. It all kind of lives here. It's not fully in the past yet. Part of that is still alive.

During the summer of 2023, Kate organized a 1980s-themed movie series in the local park. They showed *The Princess Bride* and *The Goonies* and had scheduled what Kate says was a local favorite—*Stand by Me*—to wrap it up. The film, directed by Rob Reiner, is based on King's novella *The Body* from his collection *Different Seasons*. It is a coming-of-age story of four twelve-year-old boys who hear about the dead body of a twelve-year-old boy and set out on an adventure to see it. The story is about friendship, trauma, difficult familial relationships, human strengths and weaknesses and death.

The morning I was going to show this movie I woke up and it was raining. I checked the news because the night before when I was driving home, I'd seen about thirty fire trucks and ambulances and police cars down by the river. And I found out on this day that I was going to show Stand by Me *in Lisbon Falls, Maine, on a big screen in the park that we were looking for a body in the river because there had been a drowning. And it's terrible and sad, but something about the stories tied together. The fact that we were going to show that movie and this happens on the same day. There's lots of odd things like that that end up lining up that way.*

In August 2023, police recovered the body of a thirty-two-year-old Auburn man from the Androscoggin River. Kate is clear she doesn't think the drowning had anything to do with King but relays the fact that he writes about difficult things because bad things happen. That he does not shy away from acknowledging real life scary things when writing for kids and adults.

Growing up, Kate would see King in the grocery store. She took piano lessons two blocks from his house and drove by all the time. In high school, she read some of his work. "My perspective over the past few years being here being in the shadow of it I have a deepening relationship with his work," she shares.

"Not to get too supernatural, but it feels like there's a cross-section of something here," Kate says. "I don't have a name for it or a system of beliefs about it. Like a shadow." Then she asks me how much I know about the Shiloh Chapel in Durham, the religious facility with a dark history.

"Ohhh," Maggie exclaims.

"I don't bring it up to say it's scary and haunted because of Shiloh, but somebody was attracted to this area to build Shiloh because of something about this river valley," Kate explains. "This place here. Way before Stephen King. This area has a history."

"There are layers," Maggie says. "It has high level complexities. Not like your average small town."

RICHARD PLUMMER—GRAVEDIGGER

Richard Plummer's family has been digging graves for Lisbon and Lisbon Falls for four generations. A hardworking and self-contained man, Richard was born on February 17, 1952, in Lisbon Falls and, other than a few months, has lived there his whole life. For the past forty-three years, he has owned a rubbish removal business.

I wanted to speak with Richard because King dug at least one grave when he was a kid, and I was curious what that experience would have involved. Also, King's fictional town of Castle Rock has three cemeteries. In his novel *The Dark Half*, there's a memorable character by the name of Steven Holt who is the Rock's head groundskeeper. His nickname is "Digger." And let's just say (1) you should absolutely read the book—it's one of my favorites; (2) Richard is *much* less jagged than Digger. Much more of a gentleman.

When Richard was young, he says in Lisbon Falls everybody knew everybody or knew of everybody. "It was a pretty simple easy place to live. The majority of the people were closer to poor than rich, but we never felt poor because everybody was kind of in the same ballpark. We didn't go without anything. It was different than life is today for sure."

Richard has five siblings, and until he was in high school, his mom didn't work outside the home. When she first went to work in the textile mill, she could work only six hours a day. That's all they would allow, he tells me. "So, my dad worked really, really hard," he shares. "And like I said, we never went without a thing and we never felt poor. In reality, compared to what people would consider today we were poor. Most everybody was in the same boat so we just enjoyed the simpler things of life."

Richard's mother worked at Worumbo Manufacturing until she got a job at Health-Tex Inc., manufacturers of children's clothing in Brunswick. Richard tells me with pride that she could sew, knit, crochet and even made his wife's wedding dress.

Growing Up in Lisbon Falls

"The drugstore—Robert's Pharmacy—had what we would call a soda fountain," he says. "Stools at the bar and you could get ice cream or milkshakes or ice cream floats. You could do the same thing at Kennebec Fruit. Then there were a couple of clothing stores, Robinsons and Rosenberg's, where you could actually go in and buy clothing."

His Father

Richard's father's real name was Lomimer. However, he was known as Mike. Richard tells me that when his dad was younger an older gentleman in town found out his name was Lomimer and said that's no name for a boy and you're Mike. So, he was called Mike from then on. He worked a good part of his life in the textile mills in Lewiston and then a couple different ones in the area. He dug graves on the side at the majority of cemeteries in town.

Richard tells me a number of the thirteen cemeteries in town started as family cemeteries and ended up expanding to include non-family members and that several are affiliated with churches.

Digging a Grave

Richard was fifteen years old when he dug his first grave. He accompanied his father and his uncle Frannie after they got off work.

Hillside Cemetery in Lisbon Falls. *Photo by author.*

My uncle Frannie was fun to be around and of course I loved being around my dad so if they were digging, I would go out. Needless to say, when you could help you would help. There were times when Frannie would not be available so I would help my dad. Sometimes one of my brothers would help him. It just wasn't anything I thought too much about. It was just a job and my dad whatever he did he was really particular and really good at. I feel so pleased that he taught me how to dig one right. How to consider the vault people who were going to have to put the vault in the hole and everything.

How to Dig a Grave by Hand

Richard says the first thing to know is a grave is eight feet long, three feet wide and four feet deep. The old wives' tale is they're six feet deep. "I don't know if I'm man enough to dig one six feet deep," he shares, laughing.

He uses an eight-foot-by-four-foot piece of plywood and positions it where he needs the hole and cuts around three sides of the plywood and then moves it over three feet and makes another cut. Then he uses a yardstick to cut the other lines.

What you want is when you're done you want it to look like nobody dug a hole. So, taking the sod off is the first thing that needs to be done right. In bigger places they have a machine that takes it off, but we just cut around the perimeter and then cut in one-foot strips so there would be eight of them. We used to cut down the middle so you'd have an eighteen-inch-by-one-foot strip. You'd take a flat shovel and get underneath it and slice it and take them off in pieces. We now do it in one foot by one foot because I don't know if it's acid rain or what, but sod isn't very good anymore. If you try to take it off the way we used to it falls apart. You stack that off out of the way. The next issue is you need to haul off two-thirds of the dirt to offset the vault going in.

After the grave was dug you didn't cover the hole, but for quite a number of years we have. I think the reason we started before it made sense to was we had a vault man show up and there was a skunk in the hole. You don't want to anger a skunk. Of course, it did a lot of digging trying to get out. They put a plank in, and the skunk climbed up off the plank. We started covering the holes, and now for safety we always do.

To finish the grave, once you estimate what you haul off and then we put down the canvas and pull it right up to the edge of the grave and then we dig the rest of the grave out onto the canvas. The last remaining dirt. One of the things my father taught was make sure you keep the dirt pile back roughly eighteen inches from the grave. This is because when they set up to put in the casket, they plank around it and then cover it with fake greens. That way the vault man has room to put his planks. Once the hole is dug out then we have a big enough canvas that we cover the dirt pile up. That's really important in the earlier part of the year and the later part of the year. It helps prevent the top of it from freezing.

The Perfect Grave

There was one time I was around twenty so my dad was in his late fifties and it just happened to be a perfect grave and believe it or not we dug it in just under an hour. I mean the wheel was perfect it was short quick the digging was great the sod was strong. And we didn't even talk to one another. That's the quickest we've ever dug one.

After my uncle stopped, I dug with my dad for quite a while. The last grave I dug with my dad was at Hillside and it was in November and he was seventy-two-years old. When he got out of the hole—he used a small ladder—he says, "I'm all done." And I said what do you mean and he said, "You'll have to do it now yourself, I'm done." And I said till spring? And he said, "We'll see," and he never did dig another grave with me. In fact, thirteen months later he died.

Richard dug on his own for a number of years after his dad retired. When his son came back into the area, they began digging together. "He had also dug one or two graves with my dad," Richard tells me. "So, that aspect is kind of special."

When digging on his own in the fall, as the days grow dark earlier, Richard shares he occasionally finishes up in the dark. He says it freaks some people out but doesn't bother him.

> *People react differently when they find out you dig graves. So, I sometimes like to mess with people a little bit. I've had people go, "You bury dead people," and I look at them stone-faced and say they don't have to be, but it costs more if they're not. Usually, people clam up and don't say a lot. Or they say, "I don't know how you can do that." I say I don't worry about the dead, it's the living I have to watch out for.*

Richard enjoys the physical work and says having been around the cemetery for so long he finds a sort of peace there.

"When a new vault man comes and they'll say that that's the best grave they've ever seen," he says, smiling, a glint in his eye, "it makes you feel good, because I always tell them that's just the way my dad taught me to dig them."

―――

JIM NUTTING—"BUG MAN"

Lisbon Falls was like a snow globe the day I visited in mid-February. I stepped off of a snow-covered sidewalk at 51 Main Street and into a magical world where enormous ants were crawling up a historic former church building. In the basement of St. Cyril and St. Methodius Church, a neo-Gothic landmark, there was a wall of terrariums filled with walking sticks, cockroaches, millipedes, Arizona scorpions and blue death feigning beetles to name a few.

I had gone there to meet the busiest person in Lisbon Falls at any given time, Jim Nutting, who is also known as the "bug man." He is a stained-glass artist, an amateur arachnologist, an amateur conchologist, a lepidopterist, a bibliophile, an audiophile and a collector of *National Geographic* magazines.

Jim runs weekly stained-glass workshops, restores stained-glass windows and lamps and welcomes school groups from all over Maine to his Butterfly and Insect Museum. Since 2010, he has run the Maine Art Glass Studio in Lisbon Falls, a gallery/instruction space/workroom/stained-glass supply shop.

An indefatigable man with bright eyes and a contagious excitement, he glides past an open classroom area with wide tables, fluorescent lights and a huge parrot house and settles at a table of broken Tiffany–style table lamps. Jim's gorgeous African grey parrot Polla sits on his shoulder, whistles, meows and eats the collar of his sweatshirt.

Portrait of Jim Nutting, owner of the Maine Art Glass Studio and founder of the Butterfly and Insect Museum in Lisbon Falls. Photographed with pal Polla (the parrot) and a Jackson's chameleon. *Photo by author.*

Outdoor Inspiration

Jim is committed to all things creepy and crawling. Critters that are 100 percent Stephen King worthy. He first became enamored with nature as a child growing up in Millinocket, running around in the woods behind his house. He tells me growing up in Millinocket the woods went on forever and hanging out in them was where he was happiest.

"I could literally walk from my house to Canada without crossing a tarred road," he says. "When I was a teenager, there was lumber all over. I'd scarf it up and make treehouses. Made one seven stories tall. I'd climb up and make a floor with a hole in it, build some walls, cap that with a roof and kept going up."

Born in Bangor to a school administrator and teacher, he is the oldest of eight children. The family moved to Auburn when Jim was in the eighth grade. He attended high school in Auburn and Bates College in Lewiston, where he majored in biology, graduating in 1976.

He tells me that when he was five years old, his mother was fascinated by butterflies. He caught moths she found flying around the lights and butterflies and showed them to her. She made Jim a butterfly net, and that was the beginning of his keeping insects.

Fantastic Insects and Arachnids

During a tour of the museum, Jim picks up a Chilean rose tarantula (*Grammostola rosea*), which is furry and soft and only a little intimidating.

Tarantulas have a bad rap, he tells me. Only some are aggressive. "They're huge and horrible looking," he explains. "People will be terrified, but I show them there's nothing to be afraid of. Ants creep me out more. I've been bitten by them."

Jim then demonstrates how a scorpion glows when an ultraviolet light is put on it (this does not harm it).

The tour continues upstairs with his extensive taxidermy collection of giant hornets, tarantulas (old pets), a giant walking stick, moths, butterflies and blue bees (*Xylocopa caerulea*). Jim points out that only the females are blue; the males are black.

Collecting

Jim says his father was a collector and that he's been collecting his whole life. In the old church, he has a room with shelves and more shelves of books on the natural world, in another thirty empty aquariums, in another every issue of *National Geographic* since 1920. In the shell room, he has more than ten thousand CDs in boxes and five thousand records in the bell tower. In one room, there were bags and boxes of every sort of shiny, smooth, scalloped and spiky shell you can imagine.

> *I've been collecting butterflies for sixty-three years. Seashells about as long. I've always been into anything with natural history. I'd collect moss and pinecones. I'm a hoarder. I have a friend who is a malacologist. She has written a book on shells and is going through my shell collection and is organizing it. When there's time, I'd like to create a shell museum here.*

Intro to Stained Glass

Craftschool was a part of Lewiston's downtown area for most of the 1970s. It offered visual and performing arts classes—including mime performance and Japanese woodblock printing—a public gallery and an art supply shop. In 1977, Jim enrolled in a stained-glass class taught by a friend from high school. He's been making stained glass full-time since 1998. He has clients all over the state—including private homes, the chapel at Bates College and the Lisbon Falls Community Library.

As much as he enjoys working with stained glass, he loves teaching. In the thirty-five years since he started teaching, he estimates he's had hundreds and hundreds of students from all over Maine and New Hampshire.

4

INTERLUDE
CASTLE COUNTY, CASTLE ROCK

As astounding as Stephen King's imagination is, even he has had to rely on the real world to create a believable fictive reality, borrowing freely from places he lived in during an impressionable period in his life as influenced by the horror movies and military-themed comic books he was enraptured with at the time.

Castle Rock, Derry and Jerusalem's Lot are King's trinity of fictional Maine towns. The King Universe. Castle Rock is the county seat of Castle County, which also includes such fictional places as Castle Lake and Castle View. The area known by locals as "The Rock" is home at any given time to a serial killer, a rabid dog and a demon. Derry is the longtime residence of a dancing monster clown. Jerusalem's Lot is where vampires go to party.

On Google, if you type in "places that inspired Stephen King's Castle Rock, Maine," your search should yield approximately forty-three million results. Do the same for Derry, and you should get around seven million. For Jerusalem's Lot nearly twenty-nine million.

There's just something about the town of Castle Rock that draws King readers in. Leaves us wanting to know more. It has a certain je ne sais quoi factor about it. Maybe it is because it was the setting for so many of his stories between 1979 and 1991, when he was really getting going. Or because the town is better developed than the others. Or maybe, it's just there is so much mystery to the town. It's not a secret that he used Lisbon Falls, a small former mill town in western Maine, as inspiration. But whereas Jerusalem's Lot and Derry are essentially self-contained towns in his stories,

Aerial photo of downtown Lisbon Falls taken in February 1993—including train tracks, main street, residential area. *Courtesy of Maine Home Photography.*

Castle Rock is the center of a web. Castle County is made up of almost all the other towns where characters live, work and/or travel through. And, this is important, western Maine is harder to navigate—it is out of the way. Little towns tucked largely out of reach—off the primary tourist routes. An area largely forgotten once the folks with lakeside summer homes head back to Massachusetts. It's a tougher nut to crack.

In Castle Rock, King takes readers down two-lane country roads alongside which families have built homes where children have snowball fights in the backyard and kids skate on neighborhood ponds lined by pine and spruce trees. It is the type of town where church bake sales are attended by women with perfectly coiffed hair who know everybody and their business. It is also a place where a barefoot, bare-chested man wearing moth-eaten foxtails around his neck can feel at ease while shopping on Main Street. Where the slayings are sensational and there are supernatural goings-on. In short, day-trippers beware, you have entered the dark side of the American dream. Or, as I like to think of it—Stephen King's brain.

Researching a Fictional Place

I started learning about Castle County's towns and Castle Rock's landmarks and citizens from a quartet of twelve-year-olds by the names of Gordie Lachance, Chris Chambers, Vern Tessio and Teddy Duchamp. They are the protagonists in one of my favorite King stories, *The Body*, from his collection *Different Seasons*. They play cards in a treehouse in a big elm overhanging a vacant lot in Castle Rock. The sides of the treehouse come from a scrap pile behind Mackey Lumber & Building Supply. They listen to rock 'n' roll on WLAM radio in Lewiston (real radio station and real town) and watch the Great Southern and Western Maine freight trains (based on the old Maine Central Railroad line) rumble by on their way up to Derry.

When a child goes missing in *The Body*, a search is made of Castle Rock's surrounding towns of Motton (fictional), Pownal, Chamberlain (the fictional one, because there is an actual village in a different part of the state) and Durham.

The town common is a great example of where things get tricky trying to figure out just how much Castle Rock physically resembles Lisbon Falls. King, at least in his stories through the mid-nineties, uses 1950s and 1960s Lisbon Falls to create his Castle Rock of the 1970s and 1980s. He also picks

Maine Central Railroad tracks in Lisbon Falls, which run along the Androscoggin River. Likely an inspiration for the tracks in King's novella *The Body. Photo by author.*

up buildings and streets and sets them down in different places. And it is not beyond him to change the name of a street—real or fictional—from one book to the next.

The town common looks almost exactly as King describes it in his novel *The Dead Zone*. A grammar school and the library are across from each other. Near the center of the common, there is a slight dip and a bandstand. In real life, the common dips slightly toward the center, by which there is a bandstand. Two buildings face each other. On the south end is the recreation center, which was the old Marion T. Morse Elementary School that operated between 1955 and 2005. Located on the north side is the former Lisbon Falls High School, a red brick two-and-a-half-story Romanesque Revival–style building that was converted into a grammar school in 1952. It had closed by 1985, when the building housed the school district offices.

The only notable difference is in the book the town common abuts a baseball field, whereas the real one is surrounded by quiet side streets. Also, the Lisbon Falls Library is several blocks southeast in the business district. During the sixties and seventies, half of the library—due to overcrowding of schools—was used as a sort of one-room schoolhouse for a sixth-grade class.

A Castle Rock Trilogy

The first time that readers experience the little town of Castle Rock is in King's 1979 novel *The Dead Zone*, about an emotionally tormented psychic and a sheriff searching for the perpetrator of what is called the Castle Rock Strangler serial killings. According to King, this is the first in what he calls his Castle Rock Trilogy.

King considers the short story "The Sun Dog" in his 1990 collection *Four Past Midnight* the second in the trilogy. In a note preceding the story, King writes that he felt the time had come to close the book on the town of Castle Rock.

Between *The Dead Zone* and "The Sun Dog," Castle Rock was used as the setting for the novella *The Body* and his novels *Cujo* and *The Dark Half*.

"The Sun Dog" kicks off with the remnants of fifteen-year-old Kevin Delevan's chocolate-frosted birthday cake knocking his brand-new Polaroid 660 camera onto the floor, damaging it. Photos begin showing a large black dog approaching. Delevan and his dad pop down to see Reginald Merrill, the owner of the town's illustrious antique and junk shop the Emporium Galorium. Things get funkier from there and blow sky high by the ending.

Main Street, Lisbon Falls, 1963. Local egg delivery man is leaning against his blue truck. *Courtesy of the Lisbon Falls Historical Society.*

Needful Things, published in 1991, was intended to be the last of the Castle Rock stories. A menacing stranger arrives in town, opens up a curio shop and takes advantage of the town's citizens, who are putty in his hands. Things reach boiling point, and from there it's total carnage. It's an ode to the eighties-era televangelists, small-town gossip mills and dolls that sparked riots. The town is left in ruins, but like in any great horror franchise, I guess nobody took a pulse, because sure enough the town lived to see another day.

Two years after putting out *Needful Things*, King was traveling readers back to Castle Rock again in his short story "It Grows on You" from his 1993 novella *Nightmares & Dreamscapes*. His most recent visit was in 2022 with *Gwendy's Final Task*, which he co-wrote with author Richard Chizmar. Thank goodness for best-laid plans.

Key Characters of Castle Rock

The Merrill Family

An antagonistic family whose depravity is a thread that runs through the fabric of Castle Rock. John "Ace" Merrill is a bully who appears in *The Body*, "The Sun Dog," "Nona" and *Needful Things*. He is played by Kiefer Sutherland in

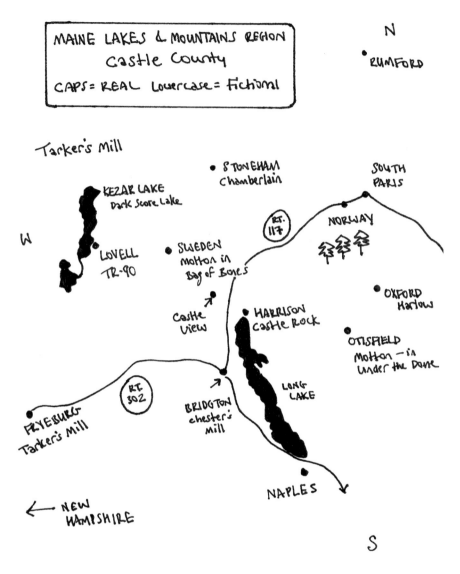

Stand by Me, Rob Reiner's film adaptation of *The Body*, and by Paul Sparks in the Hulu television series *Castle Rock*. Ace's uncle Reginald "Pop" Merrill is the predatory owner of the Emporium Galorium, a junk shop featured in "The Sun Dog." Tim Robbins plays him in the series *Castle Rock*.

THE DEVIL AND THE DOG
Frank Dodd is a serial murderer who also happens to be the deputy serving under Castle Rock sheriff George Bannerman in *The Dead Zone*. Two years

Map of Stephen King's fictional
Castle County. *Illustration by author.*

later, in the novel *Cujo*, he is the boogeyman in the closet who terrifies a
young boy by the name of Tad Trenton. King really had it in for poor Tad,
because where Dodd leaves off, a rabid two-hundred-pound Saint Bernard
by the name of Cujo takes over. Before Cujo became a monster, he was the
loveable pet of the Camber family.

Dodd and Cujo are almost always referenced in King's stories as reminders
of the diabolical horror that marks Castle Rock.

MISCELLANEOUS LAWMEN

Sheriff George Bannerman enforces the law in *The Dead Zone*, *Cujo* and the novella *The Body*. After his rather violent early retirement, he is replaced by Alan Pangborn. As the sheriff of Castle Rock, Pangborn doesn't have that much of an easier time in *The Dark Half*, "The Sun Dog" or *Needful Things*.

Andy Clutterbuck is a deputy sheriff who serves under Alan Pangborn in *The Dark Half* and *Needful Things*. He also appears in *Lisey's Story* and the short story "Drunken Fireworks." His grandfather is featured in King's short story "It Grows on You" in the collection *Nightmares and Dreamscapes*.

Norris Ridgewick is a deputy sheriff who serves under Alan Pangborn and later succeeds him as sheriff. He is described as bearing a passing resemblance to Deputy Barney Fife from the hit 1960s television series *The Andy Griffith Show*. Ridgewick appears in *The Dark Half*, *Needful Things*, *Bag of Bones* and the Gwendy books.

Tom Skerritt plays Bannerman the film adaptation of *The Dead Zone*. Scott Glenn does due diligence as Sheriff Pangborn in the series *Castle Rock*.

The Geography of Castle Rock and Castle County

Even though Castle Rock is heavily based on Lisbon Falls, that is not where it is physically located. Following are all the hints and curveballs King provides to keep us guessing about the location.

Real towns in stories: Bridgton, Brunswick, Durham, Fryeburg, Harrison, Lewiston, Lisbon, Minot, Naples, Norway, Orrington, Otisfield, Portland, Pownal, Rumford, Sanford, South Paris.

Fictional towns in stories: Castle Rock, Castle View, Chamberlain, Chester's Mill, Gates Falls, Harlow, Ludlow, Motton, Tarker's Mill, Unincorporated TR-90.

CARRIE. Chamberlain shares a border with Motton and is forty miles from Brunswick.

THE DEAD ZONE. Castle Rock is identified as the county seat of Castle County. The town is described as being considerably west of Pownal in the Lakes Region, about thirty miles from Norway and twenty miles from Bridgton. A brook is said to form the southern border between the towns of Castle Rock and Otisfield. That puts Castle Rock roughly around the town of Harrison.

CUJO. There is a reference that from Castle Rock, tourists headed toward Route 302 could turn east to Naples or west toward Bridgton and Fryeburg. Castle Rock is fifteen miles from Bridgton. That puts Castle Rock somewhere around Naples. Augusta is referenced as being two or three hours away, which does not fit with the rest of what King gives us, as Bridgton and Naples are ninety minutes to Augusta in heavy traffic.

It's also noted that Motton shares a border with Chamberlain, as well as bordering Chester's Mill (based on Bridgton) to the north and northwest.

DIFFERENT SEASONS. *The Body* puts Harlow thirty miles east of Castle Rock. Chamberlain—a town forty miles east—is surrounded by Motton, Durham and Pownal.

SKELETON CREW. "Nona": Harlow is described as being across the river from Castle Rock.

"Gramma": Castle Rock is mentioned as being just south and west of Lewiston-Auburn off Route 117. That could fit with Naples.

"Uncle Otto's Truck": Gates Falls is given as a place for last-minute holiday shopping. I take that to mean it is reasonably close to Castle Rock. *I believe Gates Falls is based on Lisbon Falls.

THE DARK HALF. A Little League field is described as being near a railroad trestle between Castle Rock and Harlow.

To avoid the Maine Turnpike, it's recommended when driving from Ludlow (based on Orrington) to/from Castle Rock to go either through Lewiston-Auburn west toward the Lakes Region or Oxford.

Castle Rock is placed eighteen miles southwest of South Paris. That could sort of fit with Naples, which is more like twenty-five miles from South Paris.

FOUR PAST MIDNIGHT. "The Sun Dog" references Harlow being next door to Castle Rock and Portland being fifty miles south.

NEEDFUL THINGS. Rumford is noted as being thirty miles north of Castle Rock. Castle Rock is placed eighteen miles southwest of South Paris.

NIGHTMARES & DREAMSCAPES. "It Grows on You" puts Gates Falls near Castle Rock.

THE GIRL WHO LOVED TOM GORDON. There is a reference to passing through Castle Rock on the way from Sanford to the trailhead, which is part of the Appalachian Trail.

EVERYTHING'S EVENTUAL. "Riding the Bullet" has Gates Falls being around fifteen miles of woods to the outskirts of Lewiston.

LISEY'S STORY. The titular character, Lisey Debusher, is from Lisbon Falls on Sabattus Road (there is a Sabattus Creek in real-life Lisbon). She is noted as having lived in Castle Rock for eight years as an adult. Specifically, the house is said to be located between Castle View and Harlow.

JUST AFTER SUNSET. "N" mentions Motton as being one town over from Chester's Mill.

UNDER THE DOME. The story is set in Chester's Mill, which is described as being surrounded by Motton to the south and southeast, Harlow to the east and northeast, Unincorporated TR-90 to the north and Tarker's Mill to the west. Route 119 (real roadway) runs through Motton from downtown Castle Rock to Lewiston. In real life, Route 119 runs between South Paris and Minot.

REVIVAL. Part of the story centers in Harlow. There are multiple references to Gates Falls being adjacent to Harlow.

ELEVATION has Route 119 become Bannerman Road inside Castle Rock's town line.

IF IT BLEEDS. "Mr. Harrigan's Phone" references Harlow and Gates Falls as being close to each other.

1960s Main Street Lisbon Falls

There's something extra special about Castle Rock's little downtown, lined with independently owned business like You Sew and Sew and a popular café by the name of Nan's Luncheonette. Following are the real-life inspirations for some of these places.

The downtowns of Lisbon Falls and Castle Rock are bookended to the north by tree-lined residential streets where town doctors and some Main

Image of snow-covered Main Street and Worumbo Mill in Lisbon Falls, late 1960s. *Courtesy of the Lisbon Falls Historical Society.*

Street shop owners live and to the south by industry and waterways, Lisbon Falls by the old Worumbo Mill and Androscoggin River, Castle Rock by a mill and the Castle Stream.

From the North End of Town

LISBON FALLS—At 11 Union Street is a building constructed in 1938 where today you'll find the coffee shop Little River Coffee. Past tenants include Anderson's Hardware store (1950s maybe into early 1960s) and a recreation hall (latter half of 1960s). Ron Huston, who grew up in Lisbon, remembers pool tables, pinball machines and a large model racetrack. The *Lisbon Enterprise*, the local weekly newspaper, was in the basement during the fifties and sixties. When King worked for the paper, it was likely in that location. At some point, the paper operated out of a nearby two-story log cabin that has been replaced by a parking lot.

CASTLE ROCK—The *Castle Rock Call*, the town's newspaper, is on the north end of town just off Harrington Street. Myrtle Harrington was a neighbor of the King family when they lived in West Durham, Maine. She gifted an old typewriter to Stephen and his brother David.

Downtown Lisbon Falls, Maine, 2023. *Photo by author.*

LISBON FALLS—The public library is located at the corner of Main and Union Streets. During the fifties and sixties, half of it was used as a sort of one-room schoolhouse due to overcrowding in the town's schools. Ron attended sixth grade in the building in the early seventies. He recalls school day mornings watching a shift of mill workers wearing Dickies work pants and carrying aluminum lunch boxes coming down the sidewalk to punch in at the mill. School let out around three o'clock, and by that time a shift of mill workers would be getting out of work and scurrying past.

The Man in the Black Suit

Ron says around the time he was attending sixth grade (1971–72) fraternal organizations—including the Knights of Pythias, Lions Club and the Improved Order of Redmen—were a part of the town's fabric. One day he was outside during recess, and a tall older gentleman by the name of Mr. Carrier went "strutting" by. Ron tells me he was wearing a top hat and black suit with long tails. He would have been an officer of one of the organizations—possibly the Free Masons, who met in their enormous two-story red brick lodge just off Main Street, or the Knights of Columbus, who held meetings in the building north of the library.

As he recalls this man in his top hat and black suit, I wonder what if King saw the same thing and that inspired his short story "The Man in the Black Suit" from his collection *Everything's Eventual*. The narrator is an old man describing an event that happened when he was nine years old in 1914. He was living in the small town of Motton and saw a man in a black suit on the bank of the Castle Stream while he was fishing.

In *Gwendy's Button Box*, which he co-wrote with Richard Chizmar, the character of Richard Farris is a mysterious stranger dressed in black and wearing a black hat.

West Side of Main Street

Lisbon Falls—Across from the library at 24 Main Street on the southwest corner of Main and Union Streets is a two-story red brick building. At some point during the fifties and sixties, the building was Crosman's Funeral Home and later a furniture store. The police station was housed in the basement in the sixties. Police officers would come and go from the back door into what is a wide alley. In King's recent novel *Holly*, the titular character's mother's funeral is handled by Crossman Funeral Home.

During the late 1950s and early 1960s, a First National chain grocery store was next door. Then the bank Depositors Trust Company. Neighboring that was Dunton's, primarily a watch and clock repair shop that also sold guns, jewelry and knick-knacks.

Western Auto

Where the Olive Pit Brewing Company resides today at 16 Main Street was once home to Western Auto. In King's debut novel, *Carrie*, published in 1974, the Western Auto Store in the Castle County town of Chamberlain goes up in flames. In his 1991 novel *Needful Things*, it's the doorway of Castle Rock's Western Auto where the character Charlie Fortin (a local drunk) smokes his "stinky home-rolled" cigarettes and watches a dangerous situation begin to unveil itself. A handyman orders a part for an air conditioner from Western Auto in King's 1998 novel *Bag of Bones*, which is partially set in Castle County.

Warren Blick "was the store" says Ron. The six-foot-plus-tall pear-shaped man is described as having been very friendly. His sister and brother-in-law (the Berniers) helped out and could be seen changing tires in the alley out back. Ron tells me that the shop was one of his favorite stops growing up in the late sixties. He recalls buying a Rawlings baseball bat and Al Kaline baseball glove there in the mid-sixties.

I'd stare at the bikes in the front window. "Stingrays" with wheelie bars, "sissy bars," chrome fenders and chainguards, fat slicks. Then I'd check out the new model airplanes from Revell, Monogram and others. Our first Matchbox cars could be goggled over in a display case and bought for twenty-five cents.

There was a hunting rifle display that always had the latest Marlin or Winchester with beautiful walnut and blue steel. The smell of garden seeds filled the air. Warren was always so nice, as well as the Berniers that worked there too.

I remember walking down to the store with my two older brothers, probably the winter of 1968–69. We had money to buy a toboggan. The snow was coming down. My brothers carried it home over their heads, and I walked between them as the toboggan was above me like a roof.

Robert's Pharmacy

At 12 Main Street where Flux Restaurant and Bar is located was once Robert's Pharmacy. Ron thinks they were there until 1966 or 1968 and then moved to another location on Main Street. In addition to the pharmacy, they had a soda fountain and sold first-aid supplies, magazines, video and audio tapes, watches, toys, candy and camera equipment. If King's grandparents needed medication, childhood neighbor Doug Hall says, that's where he would have gone to pick it up.

The shop was owned by Arthur Noyes and Rae Orline Lawrence. The business was started by Arthur's grandfather George C. Roberts in 1888. George was known for his remedies for everything from the common cold to chronic indigestion. They closed in the late 1990s. The Lawrences sponsored local youth baseball teams, and Rae and her daughter organized the first annual Miss Moxie Pageant that takes place during the annual Moxie Festival in Lisbon.

I wonder if the store could be at least partial inspiration for La Verdiere Super Drugstore in "The Sun Dog" and/or the Emporium Galorium in *Needful Things*.

End of West Side of Main Street

Next door to the drugstore was Pohle's Meat Market, then an Italian sandwich and pizza shop, which at some point became Mario's Pizza. Ron recalls going there on Sundays with his brothers and dad to pick up a pizza for the family's dinner. From Mario's, they would head down to the Kennebec Fruit Company for some Moxie.

The Kennebec Fruit Company at 2 Main Street ceased to exist in 2017 when Frank Anicetti Jr. retired and sold the building to a couple who opened Frank's Restaurant & Pub. The new owners continue to display some of Frank's Moxie memorabilia, including photos of the old store.

East Side of Main Street

LISBON FALLS—Back in the day, the north end of the business district was Bauer's Bakery at 25 Main Street, the go-to place for jelly-filled donuts. Currently, it's an insurance agency. Next door was John's Television & Appliance. Although that might have been more the 1950s than the 1960s. At 21 Main Street was at one point the location of Eddy's Men's Clothing and later a laundromat.

The space now occupied by Mike's Flooring at 13 Main Street was Rosenberg's Department Store. The shop sold ready-to-wear clothing, grocery items, sporting goods and photographic supplies. Proprietor Alfred Rosenberg inherited the business from his dad, who emigrated from Germany in the 1890s. Alfred's father peddled a pushcart and "notions," as they were called then—buttons, thread, needles, etc.—on the Portland waterfront. Eventually, he moved to Lisbon Falls, where Alfred and his siblings were born and raised. He then opened Rosenberg's store.

Among Alfred's many interests was photography, and he used to take photos from his "perch" on the front stoop of the store.

The Met movie theater closed during the late 1950s. Morse Bros. Oil occupied the end of the street in the 1950s and 1960s.

The White Elephant Barn

Located west of Main Street outside the former train station during the late 1950s was the White Elephant, an antique shop in a renovated barn. Irene Marquis, a tall French Canadian woman born around the turn of the nineteenth century who wore cat-eye glasses, ran it. This was likely the inspiration for the Jolly Furniture Barn in *The Body*—by the river and the railroad tracks.

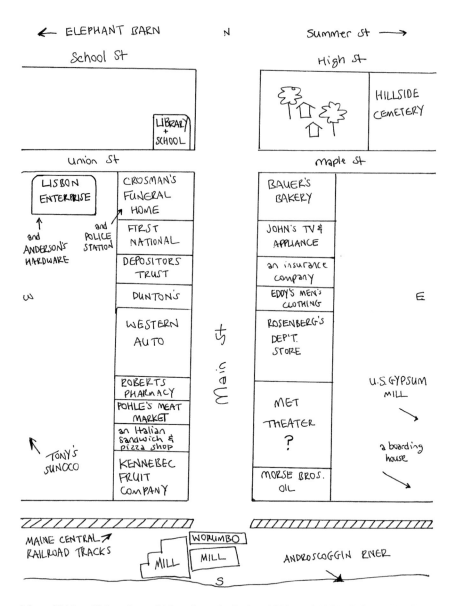

Map of Lisbon Falls as it would have been in the late 1950s and 1960s. Informed by Doug Hall and Ron Huston. *Illustration by author.*

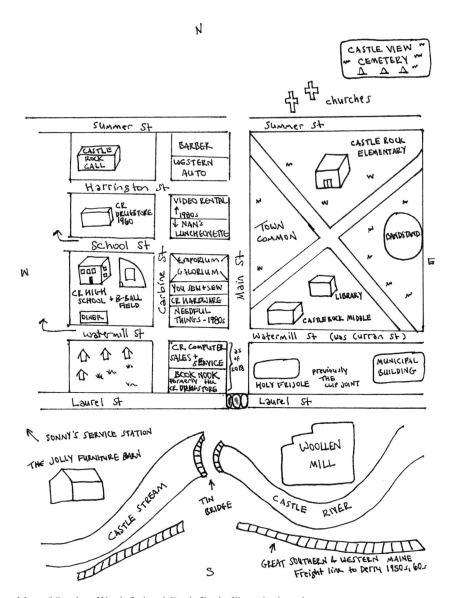

Map of Stephen King's fictional Castle Rock. *Illustration by author.*

Tony's Sunoco in Lisbon Falls

Beside the White Elephant and near the railroad tracks, Tony Martin's service station was where the wrecks in town were taken. They'd sit out back, and kids would drop by to gawk at them. Tony's also served as a tagging station during hunting season. Tony has been described as having been a wonderful man. King references a Sonny's Texaco located by the tracks in his novella *The Body*. In *Needful Things*, the Sunoco station is owned by Sonny Jackett. In *Carrie*, which is set in nearby Chamberlain, there's a Tony's Texaco. An Irving oil station and market stands at 689 Lisbon Street, former site of Tony's.

Dump Road and Richard "Eyeball" Chambers

Several blocks north of downtown is Edgecomb Road, or "Dump Road" to locals who remember when the town dump was located on it.

Ron says that when he was in high school in the mid-seventies, one of his chores was to take the trash to the dump. At the time, it was an open dump site, something that would be illegal today. People would take tires, old furniture and everything else they wanted to junk and dump it there. It was also something of a social site, attracting people Ron describes as "dump pickers" who would salvage materials and try to sell or trade them. He says he'd take his dad's van out there loaded with trash bags, and when he arrived, he'd see Richard Yenko. *I've been unable to confirm if this Richard was related to the Mike Yenko who drove the kids to school. Ron tells me Richard had what is known as a lazy eye or amblyopia, which is when one eye wanders inward or outward. Ron says Richard's nickname was "Eyeball" and has no doubt he is the inspiration for Richard "Eyeball" Chambers, Ace Merrill's best friend and the older brother of Chris Chambers.

Richard Yenko would park across from the dump and smoke a big cigar, Ron explains. He always had a guy with him whose last name was Ruby. Ron cannot recall his first name, but describes Ruby as a mean-looking guy who was actually warm and friendly and pumped gas at Tony's Sunoco.

5
MARKET ECONOMY
INDUSTRIAL EDENS: LEWISTON-AUBURN

L ewiston, about a twenty-five-minute drive from Durham, became a mythological place to young Stephen King, who went to the movies there regularly from the age of twelve to eighteen. His destination of choice was the Ritz, a two-story red brick building at the corner of Lisbon and Maple Streets. The theater was located just a few blocks from a huge textile mill complex.

The Ritz focused on monster flicks and B-movies during the 1950s and 1960s. Think low-budget Edgar Allan Poe adaptations directed by Roger Corman and starring Vincent Price, Alfred Hitchcock's masterpieces, costumed monsters preying on small American towns and apocalyptic science fiction films featuring alien ships crashing to Earth. Two other movie theaters in town were the Empire at the other end of downtown, which showed family-oriented first-run films, and the Strand, which featured Westerns.

Visiting the building today, now the site of The Public Theatre, one can imagine King walking into the Ritz, sitting down with his popcorn in the vast space in a red velour–cushioned seat, the lights dimming, the red and gold velvet curtains parting and his eyes widening as a horror story played out on the big screen.

His love of moviegoing is well documented. In *On Writing: A Memoir of the Craft*, King writes about how seeing horror and science fiction films turned his "dials up to ten."

Doug Hall, a childhood neighbor of King's, says that because King was tall for his age, he had trouble getting into the Ritz at the child's price. "The nasty lady says this kid isn't twelve, you're trying to sneak a kid in." Hall shares, "Allegedly, and I believe this to be true, my mother got a copy of his birth certificate to flash at the lady at the Ritz so that she would believe him. It was a big scene."

A scene King might have had on his mind when he sat down to write the section "Derry: The First Interlude" of his novel *IT*: Liver Lips Cole is the ticket taker at the Aladdin Theater—presumably a fictional replica of the Ritz Theatre—whom King depicts as a glaring, barking woman in a glass cage.

Tom Platz, an architect and developer, grew up in neighboring Auburn and went to the movies at the Ritz in the sixties. He explains the lobby was only ten feet deep; the bathrooms were on the right when you walked in, and you would buy tickets on the left. The concessions sold popcorn and soda. There was a small balcony. "I remember the usher used to wear the usher uniform," Platz says. "There were red velvet ropes and seating. It was old school. When you got to be older you went to the balcony with your girlfriend."

Downtown Lewiston with Basilica of Saints Peter and Paul in the distance. *Photo by author.*

Androscoggin River with old mill housing in the background. *Photo by author.*

The Bates Mill Complex in Lewiston. The redeveloped textile mill is home to restaurants, shops and housing. *Photo by author.*

The chimney of the former Bates Manufacturing Company remains a prominent feature of the Lewiston-Auburn skyline. It stands at 225 feet. *Photo by author.*

During the 1970s, when King was teaching high school English classes in Hampden, Maine, and later celebrating Doubleday and Co. publishing his first novel, *Carrie*, the Ritz—and in fact the entire area of Lewiston-Auburn—had entered a dark period.

Cathedrals of Prosperity

During the latter half of the nineteenth century and first half of the twentieth century, the metropolitan area comprising Lewiston and Auburn was the industrial heart of Maine. Four- and five-storied brick behemoths lined the canals in Lewiston, and a 250-foot-tall smokestack stood as a beacon of prosperity. On paydays, Lisbon Street sidewalks were crowded with people shopping for the latest styles in clothing in Ward's Brothers and for toys, furniture and electronics in W.T. Grant's. Five-and-dime stores were popular with boys and men buying model train kits and the latest comic books. Housewives and daughters could purchase fresh eggs, cheese, butter and tea by the pound from family-owned shops. Auburn's shoe industry produced tens of thousands of shoes weekly, and its brickyards supplied bricks for local and regional construction.

If you were young, able-bodied and wanted a good-paying job, you went to Lewiston-Auburn. The number of residents grew from 6,424 in 1850 to 64,108 in 1950. Joining Yankee ladies from area farms were men and women from the Canadian provinces of Quebec and New Brunswick.

There were so many Franco-American families in Lewiston there became a neighborhood known as "Little Canada." They started social clubs, which sponsored snowshoe races and parades. The largest was Le Montagnard with approximately one thousand members.

In 1920, the Bilodeau family bought two lots at the corner of Park and Maple Streets that had been used by a lumber dealer. They built a twenty-thousand-square-foot two-story building to use as a commercial garage. The Park Street entrance included a ramp to the second floor, where most of the repair work was done. The first floor was used primarily as a showroom for Hudson Motor Car Company vehicles.

In 1938, Manufacturers National Bank foreclosed on the property. In 1939, the Le Montagnard club purchased the building. The upstairs was turned into a clubhouse and the downstairs into an eight-hundred-seat movie theater. The latter was leased to Portland businessman Leon P. Gorman and brothers Irving and Al Cohen, who became known as the "Ritz brothers." The Ritz Theatre opened in 1940, promoting itself as "The Last Word in Theatre Comfort."

By the 1970s, as the heyday of the industrial era in the area was nearing its end, the Ritz had become a porn palace. After an erotic decade, it then sat vacant for eight years.

Renovation

In 1991, Platz, who had co-founded Platz Associates in Auburn with his brother James, was traveling to nearby cities with his wife and friends to see live theater performances. A homegrown Auburn boy at heart, he was determined to bring live theater to the Lewiston-Auburn area. Together with his friends and a group of committed citizens, they produced a performance of Beth Henley's *Crimes of the Heart* in one of the movie theaters at the dead Auburn Mall. It sold out, so they decided to do another and in 1992 rented the old Ritz Theatre to see if they could make a season of it.

Over the summer, Platz, friends and volunteers renovated the theater. After they cleared out thirty pinball machines, they removed nearly half of the seats. "The seats were a mess," Platz shares. "There was no upholstery on some and springs were popping out. I got this woman, she must have been in her late eighties, who used to work in one of the shoe shops and she taught me how to reupholster. Myself and three women took them all down in my basement and reupholstered every one of those seats, painted them and installed them. This theater was really built by the people. We had nobody to work for us and only the money we put in. That's how it started."

On October 9, 1992, Platz and friends opened what became known as The Public Theatre with a sold-out version of Molière's *Scapin the Schemer*. In 2005, the theater built on a two-story addition, installed new bathrooms, updated the wiring and plumbing and invested in a new lightboard. The theater has flourished.

Developer Tom Platz, principal of Platz Associates, which is redeveloping the Bates Mill Complex. *Photo by author.*

Interior of the Public Theatre in Lewiston. Former home of the Ritz movie house. *Photo by author.*

JIMMY AND GEORGE SIMONES, SHELLY WILLIAMS—HOTDOGGING

Jimmy and George Simones, owners, third and fourth generation
Shelly Williams, employee/bad-ass

Between fighting evil forces in Stephen King and Richard Chizmar's 2022 novel *Gwendy's Final Task*, the titular character, Gwendy Peterson, is asked by *The Washington Post* to write about five great things in her home state of Maine. In addition to Thunder Hole in Acadia National Park, the Maine Discovery Museum in Bangor, the Pemaquid Point Lighthouse Park in Bristol and the Farnsworth Art Museum in Rockland, she recommends this wonderful-smelling place called Simones' on Chestnut Street in Lewiston.

The Lewiston institution opened in 1908 as a hot dog stand with four barstools and tables made out of Coca-Cola trays. In 1966, it moved to its current location across the street, and candy-red stools and mustard-yellow booths were installed, generating a welcoming atmosphere. The walls are lined with pictures of staff with politicians, including John F. Kennedy Jr., when he was campaigning for a family member and U.S. Senator Susan Collins.

Simones' is where people of all political persuasions drop in to shake hands with the neighborhood's residents. "We're like a soapbox and you can debate," third-generation owner Jimmy Simones says. "Whatever you want to say is fine. Democracy is based on free speech. You don't have to agree with everybody."

The mainstay of the menu is the "red snapper" hot dog with mustard, onions and relish. According to Jimmy, the name "red snapper" comes from the bright red natural casing of the frank and because the casing snaps when you bite into it.

Jimmy was born in 1955 and began hanging out at Simones' as a child. He recalls how in the early 1960s when thousands of people were still employed

Since 1908, Simones' has been serving their famous red hot dogs in downtown Lewiston. Mentioned in novel *Gwendy's Final Task*. *Photo by author.*

by the mills, he'd see this huge crowd coming out at lunchtime and lining up at the stand waiting to put their order in. They had just a few minutes for lunch, he explains, so there was a lot of hustle and bustle with workers coming in, grabbing their food and heading back to work.

"The sidewalks on Lisbon Street were loaded with people," he says. "When they'd get out of first shift in the afternoon the police officers were at all the major intersections downtown directing traffic because of the amount of vehicles that were exiting and the other shifts of people coming in. Then all of a sudden, the mills went overseas and a lot less people were working and it was very noticeable."

He feels fortunate to have survived. "We've got a great clientele, a multigenerational base of customers that have come in over the years and continue to come in," he shares. "We have our regular customers, and the girls will see them coming in the parking lot and they'll start getting their food ready."

There's also a nostalgia to running a restaurant in downtown Lewiston. He tells me about going with his parents on Saturdays to the lunch counters in the downtown department stores:

> *I remember when I was little and my mom and dad and I would go down and I'd get a blueberry muffin and a glass of milk.... That would be at eight in the morning, because at quarter of nine they would open the department store. Before that they had it roped off, but people at the counter could get into the shopping area early and I would be able to go and get a toy.*

Life Is Stranger than Fiction

George, the fourth generation of the Simones family to be involved in running Simones', says the restaurant is a place where people can be themselves. Where they can feel seen and heard. Like the customers, he enjoys watching people interact. He also likes a good story.

George asks me if I'm familiar with "Bert and I," which are humorous stories often depicting Maine fishermen and woodsmen and told with a dry wit known as "Down East Maine" humor. I am not, so he explains you have to allow the story to be told at length, getting it just right. You might not get it the first time around, George tells me, but then you think about it, and all of a sudden you just start laughing so hard your stomach hurts.

I remember one day we were crazy busy. This fella comes in all dressed up in a nice suit and tie. He cuts to the front of the line and says, "I'm in a hurry, I need a cheeseburger." And it's like ok what do you want on your burger, do you want it loaded and how do you want it cooked? He says, "I want it well, well, well done." And so, the comment back was if you're in such a hurry why don't you have it rare and he kind of looked at us. Then he got his burger, he paid, he took it in his hand and put it in a napkin and put it right in his pocket and walked out. I mean, you can't make this stuff up. Wrapped it in a napkin and put it in his suit coat and walked out. It's just the crazy things that happen day in and day out.

You Could Come from Money or Come from the Dirt

Shelly Williams has been working Monday through Friday from 8:00 a.m. to 2:00 p.m. at Simones' since Thursday, August 12, 1999. She knows that date off the top of her head.

I had a job at a little corner convenience store in Lewiston and it closed down on a Sunday. I had a sister that worked here. I actually could see this place from where I lived in my apartment for eight years without coming down here. Which I almost feel ashamed, because I always thought why would I want to go out for a hot dog—not even knowing. I came in that Monday after the store closed. They needed a little help, and my sister talked to Jimmy and he said you can start Thursday. I said alright, and I've been here ever since.

Shelly says working at a place that has been a beloved part of Lewiston's food scene for decades is like the show *Cheers*, where everybody knows your name.

It's one big happy family. It's all on a first-name basis. Mayors, governors, first name. It's not like "governor" or "your honor." Everybody seems to kind of get along or everybody kind of knows each other or someone will say oh I was referred to this place by so and so. Or we don't know what their names are that come in here, but we know what they get to eat. Everybody is welcomed. Nobody acts any different than anybody else. Nobody is treated any different. You could come from money or come from the dirt; it doesn't matter.

Born and Bred Lewiston

Shelly Williams, employee/bad-ass, Simones'. *Photo by author.*

Shelly was born in Lewiston in 1968. The best years of her life, she says, were from the age of six to seventeen, when she lived in a Lewiston Housing apartment complex. "We had our own group of friends," Shelly shares. "We played a lot of basketball, because we had basketball courts, softball because we had a softball field, we'd ice skate in the winter, there were nice sledding hills right by our building. Everybody got along."

"Altogether, the people around here are so different and people definitely have their own opinion about Lewiston—especially the downtown," Shelly says. "I'd be one of the first to stand up for it. I love this town. I do. It makes it hard when people down it, and a lot of people who down it aren't even people who live around here. They come and hear stories. It has gotten worse since I lived on Knox Street, but you know everybody is pretty good."

How to Serve a Hot Dog

Shelly puts the condiments on the bottom. "When you take a bite of the hot dog and the hot dog moves, you're not going to wear the stuff that's on the hot dog," she explains. "It'll still be in the bun, it's not messy."

DON GOULET—UNDERCOVER OFFICER

Don Goulet was born in 1964. He grew up in an area on the outskirts of Lewiston where homebuilding created a big playground, because of the excavators and dump trucks and everything a kid like Don enjoyed. He says that as long as kids were home by dark or dinner, they were all over the place without the concerns there are today.

I wanted to speak with Don because of King's multidimensional small town law enforcement characters and the journeys he takes them on.

Police Chief for a Day

As a high school senior, Don signed up for a program that allowed him to shadow the police chief for a day. He toured the police department and city jail and attended a couple meetings. Inspired, he spent three summers while a student at the University of Maine at Orono in the Lewiston Police Department's reserve program. He tells me he was mostly on his own and liked walking and meeting people.

Don joined the Brunswick Police Department full-time in 1985 and served with them for over two decades.

As an auxiliary police officer and later as a full-time police officer, he had to help break up a lot of fights. Don says he learned how to fight in Lewiston, where people fought to fight and the attitude was no harm no foul. Growing up, his grandfather taught him how to defend himself, but there were rules. What he learned quickly is in a bar fight there are no rules.

> *We had sticks, but also blackjack and mace. Blackjack is a small leather pouch tip filled with lead. I learned blackjack was very effective. Hit hands, breaks fingers. I learned fancy moves never work, because it always turns into a wrestling match. My nightstick was a mental deterrent. I took it out and people would give up, because who wants to be hit by a stick. Mace didn't bother me. I was close to being immune to it, but mace would bother my partner, and they'd get as pissed as the person we were trying to arrest.*

Outside of fights, he did a lot of listening—which he says is a lot easier than fighting—and writing. "The old dragnet just the facts," he says, referring to the famous catchphrase, "Just the facts, ma'am," from NBC's 1950s police procedural *Dragnet*. He used a reporter's notebook and developed his own form of shorthand.

Trauma and Therapy

In 1990, a close friend and colleague of Don's was killed in a car accident in the process of chasing someone. "Emotionally I thought I was going crazy," he shares. He started drinking and wasn't sleeping. Fortunately, his boss got him in to see a psychiatrist who specialized in PTSD. That combined with classes to be a peer support gave him the support he needed to get mentally healthy.

Don says he'd been filing away everything he was experiencing, and when his friend died that system disintegrated. "I still have memories of events," he explains. "Still specific things about Jim's death, going on scene. I still get emotional even after thirty years. Accidents I was thinking of—this one lady died in my arms and her husband kept asking for me to help her. I was doing what I could."

He admits that he could go out on a scene and something would trigger a memory. When he gets stressed, he reminds himself to find his mental health toolbox and figure out where to put these emotions. In 2000, he learned how to sail and finds it to be very relaxing.

Undercover Agent

For three years in the late 1980s and early 1990s, Don worked undercover for an iteration of what is currently known as the Maine Drug Enforcement Agency. He says as far as he knows the agency doesn't use undercover agents anymore because it's gotten too dangerous. Instead, the agency tries to get people who have been arrested to cooperate.

A lot of the undercover work he did was in Lewiston because he knew the town and the police.

At the time he was doing undercover work, he had a big beard and moppy hair, but his identity was always a little different. Don says he used to have a working knowledge of French, enough so that he and another officer who was fluent in French pretended to be brothers from Canada. They were provided a tractor trailer with Canadian plates.

"Our investigation was focused on one thing, but it ended up going so far out of field because all the places we were going they bought us for who we were," Don shares. "We started getting people who wanted us to take guns to Canada. To the point where our bosses were like no we need you to focus on this. That was a pretty big—six months investigation and in the end all fell apart."

Don enjoyed the undercover work and learned a lot, including how to testify in court. He says it was scary the first time, but then you learn the rules of the court and how to answer questions. "Certain times when I would say well, I need a minute to think," he tells me. "I learned ways to mess with the defense attorney. To throw them off. It's like theater."

Codes

Plain English was used for intense situations where hypervigilance was needed or a number of people were involved, because it is harder to forget and everyone understands it. Don attended a street survival class, and one of the guys came up with rubbing his badge or putting his hand over his badge to indicate he was going to arrest someone. "You never know what bad guys see," he says. "If they knew a warrant was out for their arrest, they were looking to see what you were going to do."

Of course, sometimes codes don't work.

> *Quitting time was 11 o'clock at night. My partner had a rule no arrest after 10:30 p.m. because we'd get tied up and he wanted to go home. We're at a traffic stop and I see a gun in the vehicle. The code then for gun was 1032. So, my partner looks at me and I say, "1032." He said, "What." I said, "1032." "Jesus Christ, it's not even 10 o'clock yet." [Don laughs] So, I holler out, "Gun" and pull out my gun. That was thirty years ago and the story still comes up when we get together.*

After he left the Brunswick Police Department in 2006, Don worked as a captain with the Cumberland County Sheriff's Office until November 2022. He retired from the sheriff's office in November 2022. As of this writing in the summer of 2023, Don is a labor relations specialist with Cumberland County Human Relations.

———

JUDITH MEYER—NEWSPAPER EDITOR

If you must know one thing about Judith Meyer, it's that she believes everybody has a story and they are very capable of telling it. As the executive editor of the *Sun Journal* and *Kennebec Journal* and *Morning Sentinel* newspapers, she should know. Since 1990, it has been her job to hear people's stories.

When we meet, she tells me about being assigned to write about a couple who had fostered something like sixty children during their lifetime. Judith went to their home and remembers the house being tidy and efficient. She sat with them for an hour and a half and tried to drag stories out of them about their foster kids and why they felt compelled to do what they did, how it was fulfilling and so on. As she was putting on her coat to leave, thinking she hadn't gotten the story, the husband walked up and said, "You know we didn't even want to be parents in the first place." She asked him what he meant, and he said, "When my wife and I got married, we decided we were not going to have children." She thought, "That's the story!"

Their life was going to be a childless life, and then they ended up in their older years fostering dozens and dozens of children. Judith says it was one of the easiest stories she ever wrote, because he basically fed it to her on the way out the door.

The experience taught her not to go into an interview with a preconceived notion, to not ask them a bunch of questions and wait for them to answer. People would tell their stories; they just needed time.

King has written journalists into several of his works. *The Colorado Kid* features a rookie newspaper writer investigating a cold case. In *Under the Dome*, a small-town newspaper editor fights the good fight. So, I thought it important to speak with someone from print media for this book.

Stay-at-Home Mom to Reporter

A few years after moving to Maine in 1985 with her husband and two children, an infant daughter and an eighteen-month-old son, she began freelancing for the *Sun Journal*. She covered community events and selectmen's meetings, rode in the Hood dairy company's blimp for an article on the Fryeburg Fair and eventually received hard news assignments for things like car crashes and house fires. Occasionally, when her children were in elementary school, they rode along with her on assignment. One time, many years after covering a house fire, Judith says her son recalled her turning to him and his sister in the backseat and telling them she needed them on their best behavior because people had just lost everything they had.

> *I don't ever remember saying that to either one of them, but he said it was so impactful to him that that's where he was and the empathy he had. Because we could see the family standing outside their house watching it burn. I just wanted them to behave, but for him it was really a pivotal moment in loss. It offered them a perspective not just of what I do, but that people lose things in fires, people die on our roads and life is precious.*

Covering Tragedies and Fighting for the Public's Right to Know

When there is a tragedy, Judith says, "We write about the terrible thing, but we don't always write about the people and that's what always matters."

Around 2000, she was following up on a story about a mill worker who had died. Judith asked someone to look at the medical examiner's report and tell her the cause and manner of death. She found out he'd been electrocuted because he had dragged a live wire through a puddle. "Not that I am blaming him for dragging the wire," she emphasizes. "The puddle shouldn't have been there, and he died." The day after reading about it in the paper, the mill worker's mother called Judith, crying. The woman wanted to know how Judith got the information, saying she'd been calling the medical examiner's office daily for three months. Someone there, Judith says, had told the woman the information was confidential.

Here she's been told this for months and suddenly I'm a perfect stranger to her, I make a call, put it in the newspaper and that's how she learned how her son died. It was absolutely awful, and I was mad. I was disappointed in myself, because I didn't think to call and tell her. It never would have occurred to me. I would have thought she would have known. I was completely ticked off that somebody at the ME's office had strung her along like that.

Judith called the medical examiner's office and was told cause of death was only given to the press and a family's lawyer if they called, but Judith knew it was public record. She went back and forth with the medical examiner's office getting madder until finally they changed their policy to follow the law, which is that autopsy reports are public documents, although not all documents may be released if the family objects.

Judith didn't even tell her editor she was making these calls. She explains she was just reacting as a human being.

"It was a victory that shouldn't have been a fight," Judith says. "I don't remember that woman's name or know a thing about her, but I think about her all the time. It's part of what drives me to make sure that public records are accessible in a fair and equitable way to everybody who asks and that the information is as transparent as possible."

Small Towns and Bears

I just think rural people are so resourceful and independent. This is not categorically of course, because there are exceptions to everything. I just think as a rule, people who live in rural areas are accustomed to getting stuff done and I like that about them. They're also very accustomed to helping their neighbors, which I don't remember that necessarily growing up as a kid because in the city you could walk by your neighbor's house and never know who lived in there for years on end.

When Judith and her husband moved to Maine, they traded in central heating for a wood stove and bought tree-length logs they'd chainsaw and split. "We thought we were pioneers," she says. "Our friends thought we were crazy."

The first time her husband's grandmother visited from Queens, she paced in front of the picture window all night. "We were like, why didn't you go to bed," Judith recalls. "And she said well I thought a bear was going to come in the window and I was protecting you. I'm like and exactly what would you do if a bear came in the window. We were amused, and she was terrified and couldn't wait to go home."

Paper's Role in the Community?

"The cliché is that we tell stories and hold government accountable," she shares. "But the cliché is real. We tell stories and hold the government responsible."

During April and May 2013, three unrelated fires swept through Lewiston, destroying nine buildings, displacing around two hundred people and turning a town fearful. The first two fires were set by two different twelve-year-old boys and the third fire by two twentysomething-year-old guys.

In the first instance...the sense of panic had not arrived yet. This was just a fire. The neighborhood came out. The police bought a bunch of pizzas and had them delivered to a community center. A bunch of kids showed up and were eating pizza. We were hanging out there talking to people just trying to get that sense of where are you going to go tonight, because it was three o'clock in the afternoon. And we happened to capture a picture of this twelve-year-old kid eating pizza the police had bought and a police officer

sitting at the table with him. Something about that interview caused the
police officer to suspect him of lighting the fire.

The boy was questioned and confessed to lighting the fire. It seemed like a slam dunk. Then, the boy's court-appointed attorney talked to him, found out he was not read his Miranda Rights and filed a motion to dismiss.

At the hearing, as the attorneys went back and forth, Judith watched the boy's stepfather, a thirty-two-year-old man, who was at the table with him, suck his thumb. "I thought it was the weirdest damn thing, I could not get that out of my mind," she tells me. "I went back to the newsroom and asked does anybody think that's weird. And Mark LaFlamme (a reporter with the cop beat) said oh yeah, the cops say he does that all the time when he's nervous he sucks his thumb." She wrote up the story but couldn't let it go.

Through interviews and by reviewing public records and social media accounts, Judith was able to determine the stepfather had moved his family into the building because it was condemned and thus free. Repeated attempts, she says, were made to get the family to leave, but they would not and lived in squalor without heat or water.

Furthermore, Judith explains, the stepfather relied on the boy to babysit his three younger siblings, including an infant sister.

He's scrounging for food; he doesn't know where to get diapers. He's basically
in charge of his family. He's not going to school. The truant officer is
visiting and there's all this stuff swirling around. He felt it was hopeless.
He didn't set the fire because he was some mastermind who wanted to see
something burn. He set it because he wanted him and his sisters and his
mother to move into a different apartment and not have Charles Epps come
with them. In his mind, it was the only way.

Ultimately, the charges against the boy were dismissed. He was taken from his family and adopted and, according to Judith, became captain of his football team, was on the honor roll and went to college.

Judith stresses she does not defend what the youth did but describes his setting the fire as an act of desperation by a boy living in impossible circumstances. "I wrote this story about a kid caught in this terrible situation, the cops failing to read the Miranda to him, the city failing to enforce this eviction to get this family a place to live that was safe and warm and inhabitable," Judith says. "The government failed this entire family, and this kid was a victim but also did something he should not have done."

We have this desperate twelve-year-old white child who was wronged by police and city government in too many ways to really understand, who had a great lawyer and his case was dismissed and he went on to an amazing life and will have all the advantages available to him. Then we have this twelve-year-old Black child who the police did read his Miranda, his case was moved through the juvenile system, he goes to Long Creek. He hasn't been to school, he hasn't had a lot of contact with his family, he hasn't had any great mentors and he is going to be in the criminal justice system for the remainder of his life. It is literally black and white.

STEVE BOUCHARD—LIBRARIAN

Stephen King has a nearly lifelong love of libraries. They allowed him access to books when he could not have afforded them and nurtured his passion for the written word. The Stephen and Tabitha King Foundation has given generously to libraries across Maine.

In Lewiston, library card holders have access to nearly 160,000 items, genealogy resources, crafting circles, study rooms, book clubs, yoga classes and computers. As an adult services librarian at the Lewiston Public Library, and someone who spent a lot of their childhood there, Steve Bouchard understands the profound impact a library can have on a child's life. "It's been such a well-loved part of this community for a really long time," he says.

My parents were not college educated; we didn't travel much. The library was really the thing that opened up the world to me and showed me there was a bigger wider world out there and made me curious about the world. Just how things worked and what the possibilities were. The library was very important to me. When you're a kid you can't believe all the (free) books. It's almost too good to be true. All these books are here and they are for us and we can take as many home as we want.

Steve is from a Franco-American family, like a lot of people who were born and raised in Lewiston. His parents were bilingual, and when they went to school, until the eighth grade they went to Catholic school. He shares that the school had classes in French for part of the day and English for part of the day. Steve explains that his generation was the first generation to go to school entirely in public school. "You spoke French just a little bit when we were very, very young, but by the time we got to school we were speaking pretty much entirely English," he says. "We sort of grew up with a sense that we were from an ethnic family but were also sort of in the process of you know—my generation was becoming pretty much assimilated. It wasn't until later when I went away that I sort of really started to understand how much growing up here had kind of informed who I was."

In high school, Steve went to Germany for a year as an exchange student. Living in a foreign country in a foreign culture for a year, he says in some ways he learned more about himself and his own background during that experience. It made him interested to know more about his heritage, so when he got to college, he did an independent study project on Franco-American history. "Until then I'd known quite little about my ethnic background," Steve shares. "That was an opportunity to learn a lot more about that."

Deciding to Become a Librarian

When he graduated from college in the late 1980s it was in the midst of a recession.

It was that big recession where thousands and thousands of middle managers across the country who had thought that they were going to have secure jobs until retirement were suddenly being laid off. It was kind of a transformation recession. The job market was changed in fundamental ways, and I graduated into that market with a multidisciplinary liberal arts degree in social sciences.

Steve found himself considering his situation. Like, OK what do I do with this, how am I going to make a living, what am I going to do for work, how am I going to pay rent.

He remembers thinking very abstractedly about what interested him. Steve thinks he was doodling when he wrote those things down and what they have in common and where they intersect. "Suddenly it's like a light bulb went off in my brain and I was like libraries, that's the place where they intersect," he explains. "It almost sounds too perfect to be true.

Almost like one of these epiphanies that you read about." He looked into and eventually pursued a master's degree in library science and says it's felt right ever since.

Steve works directly with patrons; manages collections; orders materials; and does administrative work, strategic planning, space management and a whole lot more. He loves the variety, being surrounded by books and everything the library offers the community.

Although a self-described nonfiction guy, Steve tells me that he first read Georges Simenon after hearing about him for decades. As Steve is someone who reads a lot about books and book reviews and literary criticism, Simenon's was one of those names that kept coming up over and over again. When Steve came across one of his books in a remainder catalogue, he bought it, read it and says he enjoyed it. Simenon, he shares, is like a French Agatha Christie. He is known for his detective stories about a police superintendent named Jules Maigret. "They're short, but they're intense," Steve says. "He doesn't waste a word and he really kind of examines the psychology of his characters."

———

6
COMPANY TOWN
RUMFORD-MEXICO

n the early 1970s, Stephen King's older brother, David, and his family lived in Mexico, Maine, the town where their mother, Nellie Ruth Pillsbury, spent the last months of her life.

King mentions Rumford, which sits across the Androscoggin River from Mexico, in his short story "Uncle Otto's Truck" from the collection *Skeleton Crew* and in his novels *Needful Things* and *Lisey's Story*.

In his novel *Bag of Bones*, King travels protagonist Mike Noonan west from his home in fictional Derry—based on real-life Bangor—to his lake house in fictional TR-90, based on real life Lovell. Rather than take the faster route on I-95 South, King has Noonan get off the highway for a meal in Rumford and take US Route 2 most of the way. King is giving readers a map of *his* Maine when he does this.

US Route 2 is a two-lane blacktop road that is the principal east–west route in the state. It has long been used by logging trucks bringing logs down from northern Maine to sawmills and paper mills in western Maine. The miles of US Route 2 also tell stories of University of Maine students heading home to dying mill towns, of shadowy pot dealers and their clients' meetups and outdoor recreationists en route to do some fishing.

Welcome to Rumford

The first time I took in Rumford it was a dazzlingly sunny early fall day. I stopped at the visitor center by the town's waterfall—Rumford Falls—and took the obligatory photos of the statue of Paul Bunyan and his pal Babe the Blue Ox. Inside a volunteer welcomed me and told me about influential Rumford-born politician Edmund Muskie, who authored several major environmental bills, including the Clean Air Act of 1970 and the Clean Water Act of 1972. At the time of the signing, the Androscoggin River was one of the most polluted rivers in the country due to industries dumping tons of waste into it. Today, it is one of the cleanest rivers in Maine.

The picturesque main street is largely a collection of closed stores with empty shelves and beat-up restaurants. A few miles out of town, one can see the mill's smokestacks emerge out of the valley, the visible identity of the town, spewing a rotten egg–like smell 24/7, which is more pronounced depending on which way the wind is blowing. In *Bag of Bones*, King references this smell as a hellish one.

Paper-Making King

Self-made paper manufacturing magnate Hugh Chisholm established himself with the opening of the Rumford Falls Paper Company in 1901. Within its first few years of operation, the company secured the contract to manufacture the millions of postal cards used by the U.S. Post Office daily.

In the first decade of the twentieth century, the population of the towns of Rumford-Mexico swelled from 4,586 to 8,842, transforming them from a rural community to an industrial center.

Almost from the time Chisholm first visited Rumford, he emphasized investing in the community. In 1906, he engaged the services of celebrated architect Henry J. Hardenbergh to design the two-story brick-and-concrete Rumford Falls Power Company's headquarters at the southwest corner of Congress and Exchange Streets. A Historic Preservation survey conducted in 1979 states, "Built by the company primarily responsible for initiating the phenomenal development of Rumford, this flamboyant structure expresses the enthusiasm and optimism of this then burgeoning community." In 1907, Hardenbergh's French Renaissance château-style Plaza Hotel opened on Fifth Avenue in New York City.

In 1911, Chisholm and the mill financed the building of the Rumford Mechanics Institute across the street from the Rumford Falls Power Company. The facility, a block-long decorative four-story brick building with Doric columns along the front, was established as a place where residents could recreate and lend structure to intellectual growth and

The Rumford pulp and paper mill was founded as the Oxford Paper Company in 1901 by Hugh Chisholm. In 2018, ND Paper purchased it. *Photo by author.*

moral development. The building housed a lounge with a grand fireplace, a smoking and card room, a billiard room, a writing room, a lecture room, a ladies' parlor, a gymnasium with a running track and a bowling alley, in the basement.

Today, the building is used as the Greater Rumford Community Center and hosts after-school sports programs, adult boxing classes, youth basketball games, a gymnastics academy and a fitness center.

Brick Park

Strathglass Park—known as "Brick Park" by locals—is one of Chisholm's most significant contributions. It is a neighborhood of fifty two-story red brick duplexes with slate roofing considered by the National Trust for Historic Preservation to be one of finest examples of industrial worker housing in the country. The neighborhood, which is surrounded by a granite stone wall and gateway, was conceived and funded by Chisholm in 1902 as housing for mill workers and their families. It is named after his ancestral home near

The Strathglass Building, a reminder of Rumford's past economic prosperity. The grand Beaux-Arts limestone building was commissioned in 1906 by paper manufacturing magnate Hugh Chisholm. *Photo by author.*

the Strathglass valley in the Scottish Highlands, and the streets bear Scottish names like Lochness Road.

The once grand neighborhood has worn concrete sidewalks, rotting wood porch railings, littered weedy front yards and boarded-up windows.

Gary Dolloff, who was born and raised in Rumford and manages the Greater Rumford Community Center, says that when he was growing up Brick Park was the place to be. He believes the neighborhood really began to change in the nineties. "Then it became the hey you can buy a cheap house there," he explains. "You can sell your house, and somebody would come in and scoop it up and rent it. Instead of people owning, people would buy to rent."

"They used to be so nice," Mary Ann Fournier, adult services and reference librarian at the Rumford Public Library, shares. "When we were little, that was the place to go trick or treating. Fog lights and everything. It became low-income housing and a lot of the drug addicts moved there. And a lot of people like my dad who worked at the mill retired and don't live in town anymore."

A Cautionary Tale

Hugh Chisholm passed away in 1912. His presence lives on in Maine with a marble bust in the lobby of Rumford's town hall and an impressive granite mausoleum resembling a Roman temple in Portland, Maine's Evergreen Cemetery.

During his grandson William Chisholm's brief run as company president, the Mechanics Institute was turned over to the town, and manufacturing modernization eliminated hundreds of jobs. In 1967, he sold the company to the Ethyl Corporation, which sold it to the Boise Cascade Corporation in 1976 along with 335,000 acres of timberland.

A decade later, the mill experienced its worst strike, straining the town to near breaking point. Global competition and government regulations had put pressure on paper mills, and mill owners responded with changes the United Paperworkers International Union did not feel were safe for workers. During the summer of 1986, about 1,200 union members walked off their jobs.

Generations of families that had relied on a steady paycheck faced uncertain times. "The mill was sort of the center of the community as far as working," Sue Marshall, head librarian at the Rumford Public Library, tells me.

The Rumford Commercial Historic District comprises thirty-eight downtown buildings. *Photo by author.*

Gary Dolloff was stationed with the U.S. Army in California at the time but came home to visit family—including two of his brothers who worked at the mill and were striking. He says it was really bad, with people throwing rocks and spray-painting people's houses and jumping on someone's car when they went into the mill.

> *My town was a wreck. The mill brought in goons from out of town. It was tough. As the strike went on, people had no money coming in and they'd cross picket lines and that turned this town sour. Brother against brother. It was definitely a sad point in the history of Rumford. You're standing next to this guy one day and you're both picketing and fighting for your rights as a union worker and the next day he's not there. He's crossed the picket line, and it's somebody you grew up with, who you went to school with. Their excuse was I need to provide for my family, and they both look at it two different ways.*

By the time the strike ended in mid-September, around two hundred workers, many of whom had several decades of experience in the mill, had been replaced by people from outside the area—some of whom had never worked in a paper mill. What was once a close-knit community was deeply

View of the Rumford Mill. As of August 2023, 530 people are employed there full-time. *Photo by author.*

wounded. Families left the place where they'd grown up, where their parents had grown up, to start over somewhere new.

In *Bag of Bones*, King references the paper-driven economy halting in the mid-1980s.

———

GARY DOLLOFF—HOMETOWN SUPERHERO

Gary Dolloff, a comic book-worthy superhero living in Rumford, Maine, spends days in his office on the second floor of the Greater Rumford Community Center responding to calls and texts about everything from a pair of sunglasses left behind during a basketball game to someone needing help finding a refrigerator. The woman tells Gary she's been looking for a small one and can afford a little bit, but not a lot. The work of a superhero is not always easy or glamorous, but helping people who have fallen and need a hand up is something Gary has been doing gratefully since around 2008.

He has helped the Rumford Public Library secure picnic tables and put oil in neighbors' tanks. Assisted with an electric bill here and there and put food on the table. He organized a home-building project for a handicapped neighbor and has planned fundraisers. Gary's superpower is putting himself in the middle of people who want to give stuff away and people who need stuff, making a difference in his town one act of kindness at a time as manager of the community center.

When Gary was growing up, his favorite superhero was the Batman. "He was the coolest," he says. For fun he got a magnet of the Batman symbol—the bat emblem in black on a yellow background encased in a black oval—for his black Ford F-150 pickup truck. However, it kept falling off. When it was attached, he shares, "Kids would be mesmerized, adults would smile." He decided if it made people happy it was something he wanted to commit to, so he had the Batman insignia permanently painted on his car in multiple locations.

"I feel like, looking back, I was this super shy kid in high school," Gary explains.

When Adam West was Bruce Wayne—actor who played the Batman in the iconic 1960s television series—he was more reserved and I could relate to that. I couldn't speak to a girl in high school. I couldn't do it all. As time went on, I got better and better. Growing up I was the youngest of eight. The conversation always started from oldest to youngest. I would get my two words in, but that was about it. The Batman thing I felt like that was a piece of me. I could relate to him. You know, Rumford is its own Gotham. People call it Little Gotham.

That Rumford's nickname would come from the fictional, gritty, hard-hit former industrial hub in DC Comics' comic books where the Batman lives doesn't surprise me.

You come down over that hill at night and it is a different planet. It's crazy. You can see all the lights and the stacks. You go from darkness at the top of the hill, and you come down and its wow. You've got the waterfall right next to you. I take it for granted, because I'm here all the time. But I can imagine if it's somebody's first time and coming over that hill at night when the water is raging it's pretty wild.

Growing Up on the Farm

Gary was born in 1965. When he was six, his mother was killed by a drunk driver. He and his siblings were taken to live on their grandparents' farm on the edge of Rumford. Gary says he watched his grandparents struggle trying to raise eight kids on one income from the mill.

"I think being raised here and being raised by my grandparents taught me a great work ethic," he shares. "I think because I was raised by my grandparents my values were older. How to talk to people, make sure you look them in the eye and put your hand out. All the small things I think count a lot, but are kind of disappearing into the fabric."

Gary Dolloff. Hometown hero and manager of the Greater Rumford Community Center. *Photo by author.*

Gary recalls his grandparents trying to get help from the state to put food on the table. "We could get two boxes of cheese (from the government) and I just remember how much I loved that cheese. It was so good. It was the big blocks and you could cut it."

The family also received powdered milk, which he hated. Gary's grandmother would mix regular milk with the powdered milk to make it go farther and try to pass it off as regular milk, but Gary was not fooled. When his oldest brother was hired at a dairy farm down the road, he would bring milk home. Gary was also not a fan of milk right from the cow. "When she bought regular milk, everybody wanted some," he shares. "I like regular whole milk. I probably drink a gallon a week."

During planting season, Gary and his siblings would remove rocks from the field to prevent damage to machinery. "My grandfather would get on the tractor and start the rototiller up and we would follow," he says. "We'd be in lines and pick up the rocks as we went along and chuck them."

The kids also helped harvest the vegetables, which were stored in the dirt-floor root cellar below the house.

It was pretty sketchy. In the basement there was the washer, dryer, and furnace. You'd go around all that stuff and there'd be this door. It was one of those creaky old doors. It was a handmade door like you'd see in a horror movie. They'd send you down for a bucket of potatoes and [there was] that one light you had to reach up and grab and turn on. To this day it was one of the sketchiest places ever.

Mill Town and Seeds of Mistrust

Gary's grandfather did maintenance for the mill and later the wastewater treatment facility. "You didn't question what was going on with the mill," he shares. "That was my grandfather's livelihood. What put food on the table. He'd literally go to work on a Tuesday and come back on a Thursday and work that long. He had a place he could take a nap here and there, and we just needed the money."

In 1989, three years after the big mill strike, Gary returned from California, having finished his army service, and went to work at the mill. He says because he had not been around, people at the mill didn't know who he was. "They saw me driving around the mill and they thought oh that must be a scab," he explains. "The scabs in town were still treated badly. You wanted to make sure you got your name out there hey I wasn't a scab. I went into the hotel (a local bar) to visit my brother and then people knew I was local."

Gary worked for the mill for around eleven years until he was seriously injured in 2000.

We were doing an acid wash. You put acid in the tank and put water in so you can clean the sides of the tank off. At that point in my career, I had done that job then got a different job. That day someone had to do some training so they asked me if I could do that job till the kid came back. Things started going sideways. I put the acid in and it was bubbling up, and at the same time there was a smudge fire. They were welding and sparks hit the wood. There were people trying to put that fire out and the acid was getting in the grates and I'm trying to dilute it and the next thing I know I'm out. I woke up in the ambulance.

He ended up in a hyperbaric chamber at Central Maine Medical Center in Lewiston. Lingering effects included a seizure disorder and memory loss.

"In my head I felt like everything was white and I was on this white merry-go-round spinning and then all of a sudden it stretched and I woke up," he recalls of his near-death experience.

After several months, he returned to work at the mill. "I went back because that's what you do and I think that's just part of my upbringing," he says. "I would go into the place and I wouldn't feel good so I'd go down to medical and they started giving me, I don't know what it was, but a shot and it kind of put me to sleep for a while. Then I'd feel better and I'd get up and go home. That was basically my life for a while." During that time, he got divorced and tried to do the best he could for his two daughters.

Paying It Forward

It wasn't until a few years later, when in 2006 his eleven-year-old nephew Lucas passed away in a freak accident, that he set out on his path to pay it forward.

Gary says he remembers sitting in the hospital corridor with his brother waiting for Lucas's mother to arrive.

Hearing her come in was the worst thing I've ever heard. Afterwards, I went outside and hollered at God for a long time, [asking] why would God let that happen. Then the night before the funeral I woke up in the middle of the night and I started writing, writing, writing. I think that's when my life changed. Right then at that point. I woke up the next morning and asked my brother if I could speak at the funeral. And I spoke and I didn't recognize the words but it was a whole different meaning for me turning things around.

Gary tells me he wrote about keeping family close, about making sure you do right by people, hold people accountable and tell them you love them. After the accident, he explains, it was about surviving. With Lucas he realized he wanted to help people.

"I helped eight families with Christmas the first year," he says. "Then I started playing Santa Claus. When I was a kid, we would each get three gifts at Christmas, which was awesome. Then one year Santa Claus showed up with this giant bag and had five toys apiece for us in that bag. I never found out where that came from, whether this was an organization. I remember the feeling I had when they came in and I wanted to give somebody that feeling. Now I play Santa Claus on a regular basis."

―――――

SUE MARSHALL—HEAD LIBRARIAN

The woodwork, windows, everything in the library fascinates Rumford Public Library head librarian Sue Marshall. Built in 1903 with a $10,000 donation from steel magnate Andrew Carnegie, the Romanesque Revival–style building designed by architect John Calvin Stevens is on the National Register for Historic Places.

In 1969, a four-thousand-square-foot addition was built, more than doubling the library's footprint. In recent years, the Stephen and Tabitha King Foundation gave the library $45,000 to restore the reading room ceiling.

In addition to books, the library provides access to printers, a maker space complete with a 3D printer and a Cricut machine for scrapbookers and virtual reality equipment. Jungle animals are painted on the walls of the children's room, which has toys, book-cassette read-alongs and educational games. The library holds poetry meetings and a mystery readers group. The staff decorate the front desk and sometimes dress up for holidays.

Childhood

Sue Marshall is everything a librarian should be. She is resourceful, passionate, loves books, is extremely conscious of keeping costs down for patrons and encourages people to leave her bibliophile's domain with an armful of books. She also ardently defends the right to stock banned books. "Books are really expensive, so people can come here and it's one of the few places they do not have to spend money," she says.

Sue grew up in Rumford Center, outside town off Route 2, in a close-knit farming community. Her early childhood was spent playing softball with kids, some of whom worked on their family's farm. "Growing up we all went to the same school so we knew each other," she shares. "In the summer, baseball teams were very very competitive. Rumford Center and other Rumford teams had our own sports out there. Other than that, it was one big community."

"Our mothers would release us in the morning and maybe give us lunch in the afternoon and we wouldn't be home till suppertime when our dads came home from the mill," Sue says.

"We had one vehicle, and my father took it to work [at the mill] every day," she explains. "So, we were stuck out of town unless my mother got up very early to give him a ride to work and then come back and get us ready for school. If she wanted to do anything it was kind of a process and then she'd have to go pick up dad at the end of day."

Sue's father and his siblings grew up in the Rumford area and stayed. "A lot of big families stuck together and looked out for each other," she shares. There were not a lot of after-school programs when she was growing up in the 1960s and '70s, and Sue says she and other kids relied on their families and neighbors to help out.

"Downtown has changed a lot," Sue adds. "Used to be downtown was the place to be. Congress Street used to have a lot of smaller stores like variety stores. They had a little bit of everything, candy counter, arcade games. Those don't exist anymore. Lewiston was a huge event. We didn't go often growing up." The big thing in the early 1970s, she says, was the Mammoth Mart, a New England discount department store chain. The Walmart Supercenter in Mexico, she thinks, sucked people out of downtown.

Becoming a Librarian

Sue was a nurse's aide during high school. After graduating in 1978, she worked at the Rumford Community Hospital for almost twenty years. Feeling the need to reinvent herself, she went back to school.

"When I was growing up, the biggest employers were the mill or the hospital," she says. "You worked at one or the other. I never worked in the mill here. When I was getting my degree, I did work in the mill in [nearby] Jay in the summertime. My husband worked there for forty-six years. The mill would hire children and spouses of people in college so they could help area students make money in the summer."

One day, a school administrator told her about their library program.

I am a voracious reader. I will read anything. I was the kid who used to read the cereal boxes at the breakfast table just to have something to read. I said that's great right up my alley. He said jobs are scarce. I went home thought about it and told my husband I'm taking a leap. I'm going to do it. I got my bachelor's degree in library information and technology systems. I was hired within a month of graduating. I started as a library aide here then I was the children's librarian for quite a while then our director left and I moved in there temporarily and started to make it permanent.

*Sue retired after eighteen years at the library a few months after this interview.

———

MARY ANN FOURNIER—LIBRARIAN

That's not a flower Mary Ann Fournier has tucked between her locks. That is a hairpin that is a miniature replica of the bloodied axe iconized in Stanley Kubrick's horror film *The Shining*, based on Stephen King's novel of the same name. For those unaware, Jack Nicholson's character has a bit of a breakdown in a remote snowed-in Colorado hotel and engages an axe—in the book it's a roque mallet—in an altercation with his wife. Mary Ann tells me she'd been in Colorado the week of Halloween a couple years earlier to visit her uncle and they'd visited the Stanley Hotel (no relation to Kubrick). The hotel is legendary for having inspired Stephen King's novel after a brief stay there.

Mary Ann shares she also loves Carrie White, the complicated anti-villain of King's novel *Carrie*. A bullied, friendless girl with an abusive religious fanatic for a mother and maturing telekinetic powers, Carrie finally ruptures and takes her revenge in a big way.

"Carrie is scarier because of the fact that as somebody who didn't have a great high school experience, it's that thought that if I had the ability would I do the same thing as Carrie or not," she says. "Which is terrifying." Still, she rooted for her the whole time.

Background

Mary Ann was born in 1989 in Portland, Maine, where her mother is from. When she was little, the family moved to Rumford, where her father's family is from. She describes Rumford as being a safer place back then.

While studying for her degree in linguistics, Mary Ann says, "I focused on fairytales and how we use them to evolve our own language around the deceased and dying." She adds, "This is going to sound morbid, but I'm interested in the culture of death."

"People put way too much negativity around death," she shares. "Some people do it purposefully to try and get that jump out of you. Yes, it can be scary, but also beautiful. It's a dirty word, and I don't like that."

After a day of cataloging books and planning library programs, she takes online mortuary science courses with the goal of one day working in a funeral home—ideally, one in Rumford, so she could live in the house where her grandfather grew up and renovated. "In a small town, there's not as much opportunity for stuff, and that still holds true," she says. "I'd like to stay here, but I'm definitely going to have to move."

7
BORDERLANDS
LAKES REGION: BRIDGTON

Bridgton is a town with a monster story. In the beginning, there was only the beast. In early October 1886, a sheep was found slaughtered in a local cornfield. Wild animal attacks had happened before, so presumably not much notice was taken. Then on the night of October 15, a farmer on his way home heard a cry that rose to split the night. Something large and dark burst out of the woods onto the road beside him. He turned and ran for his life, tripping over a stone wall and injuring his shoulder. The beast did not follow him into the open field, and he reached his house babbling in terror. The *Bridgton News* headline the next day read "Hell Fell" and described the encounter.

Over the next seven years, more livestock were killed, and dogs went missing. Strange footprints were found. Bodies were dug up. Nocturnal shrieks were occasionally heard in the woods. A visitor traveling a road alone during the day said he saw a monster. Another traveler told of his carriage being chased by a strange animal. An old woman drove the beast away from a boy. Notices were posted cautioning people about the elusive creature.

In 1893, a road was found stained with blood, and a local butcher said he saw the beast lurking in the woods. Eyewitness accounts began to accumulate. A four-legged creature estimated to be three feet long and one and a half feet tall, it was described as part wild cat with dark vertical stripes, a hairless rat-like tail, with a wolf-like face and terrifying human-looking eyes. Mountain men who hunted bobcats and mountain lions had never seen anything like this.

By 1895, mothers had begun using old tales of the beast as warnings to keep their children out of the woods at night. The same year, the creature became known as the infamous Woolfaboomis—a colloquial term in Bridgton folklore for things that "go bump in the night." And then it was gone. Killed, grown old or gone north.

Whispers of the beast living in one of the caves on Mount Henry, a small mountain near the center of town, remained well into the 1940s, after which its presence faded into the background. That is until the Bridgton Historical Society's Mike Davis came across a story in an old edition of the *Bridgton News* in 2022 and began researching the legend's history. Whether the beast was a mutation of some sort Mike has not been able to establish.

Mike enjoys talking about the area's past. His purpose is not just to educate people about what came before but to revive it. Since 2019, he has written the column "In Ye Olden Times" for the *Bridgton News*, bringing to life former stories from historic editions of the paper.

In Mike's view, legends and ghost stories ought to be presented alongside known events to give a full picture of a small town's history. "History is as much a record of our culture as it is a list of dates and facts," he says. "More often than not our local legends, besides being sadly unknown to our modern citizens, are truly interesting histories which provide meaningful insight into our forefathers who believed in them."

The Body Snatcher

A charming lakeside town in what is known as the Lakes Region of western Maine, Bridgton sees a constant stream of visitors and second home owners between Memorial Day and Labor Day weekends. They come for the boating, swimming and area summer camps.

From the mid-eighteenth century through the first half of the twentieth century, however, Bridgton was predominantly an industrial center. The sawmill, corn packing plant, iron foundry and baseball bat making business all closed at varying points beginning in the 1930s. A shoe factory from the nineteenth century held on into the 1990s.

Evidence of Bridgton's commercial past can occasionally be found in a swampy area off Main Street that was used as the town's dumping ground from the mid-1800s into the 1960s. Tin cans, oil buckets and bottles are still working their way to the surface. Mike says the swamp has always been fertile ground for bottle pickers. Bridgton Beverage, a soda bottler that operated in town from the 1920s through the 1940s, disposed of its bottles there.

In the 1960s, a woman was bottle hunting in the old town dump and found a skull. The police exhumed the body and believed it to be at least one hundred years old. It also showed signs of having been medically dissected. Mike presumes the body was one procured by Dr. John H. Kimball, a prominent surgeon whose home was just up the hill from the dump in the 1860s. The doctor was believed to be a body snatcher who procured skeletons for doctors he was training.

In 1869, Dr. Kimball's neighbors reported hearing hammers and saws all night one night, and the next morning it was discovered the body of an old man had been stolen from the cemetery. "People put two and two together—believing he had been skeletonizing the body—and gathered outside his house," Mike explains. "He had a wagon tear out to another part of town as a distraction. Meanwhile, his accomplices hid the body somewhere in town. A year or two later, a patient of Dr. Kimball turns the entire story into a folk ballad."

Can you see why King might be drawn to this town?

Stephen and Tabitha King and their children Joe and Naomi lived in Bridgton from the summer of 1975 to about mid-1977, shortly after son Owen was born. They would have already been familiar with the area, having rented a home about thirty minutes south on Sebago Lake in North Windham in late 1973 and early 1974. That's where he wrote *Salem's Lot*. In Bridgton, King finished writing *The Stand* and wrote *The Dead Zone*.

In the latter book, George Bannerman, the sheriff of (fictional) Castle County, sits down with protagonist Johnny Smith, a man with psychic abilities, at (fictional) Jon's Restaurant in Bridgton. Over a bowl of "damn good" chili, Sheriff Bannerman asks Smith for help identifying a local serial killer. Mike thinks the inspiration for the restaurant where they met could have been Ricky's Diner, which shuttered during the pandemic. He says it was known for having very good chili.

The Shining's World Premiere

Per King's request, in 1980 the town's Magic Lantern movie theater hosted the world premiere of the film adaptation of his novel *The Shining* to benefit a local hospital. The story is about a family who are winter caretakers of a haunted hotel in an isolated area of Colorado.

A beloved neighborhood institution, the original three-hundred-seat theater opened in 1929. Mike tells me it was originally built as a car garage. Unfortunately, the cement structure was built on top of an old tannery, which had been built on wetlands, thus providing a recipe for foundational disaster. The walls sagged and cracked, and the floors buckled. By the time it closed in 2005, Mike says you could set a marble down on one end of a room and it would roll to the other end. The building was torn down in 2007 because it was literally falling in Steven's (no relation to King) Brook. It was rebuilt on the same site.

Gary Gomes, King's Bridgton-based barber, tells me during pre-pandemic visits to town King would attend the theater's weekly cribbage tournaments. Gary says he enjoyed playing against an eighty-something-year-old woman.

Write What You Know

The power of King's fiction is his ability to combine his real-life experiences with fantasy. He has mined Bridgton, where we've established some weird stuff happens, for a number of his stories.

"The Mist" (1980)
After a wild storm batters their town, a father and son head out for supplies and run into a supernatural mist in downtown Bridgton. Real-life Food City supermarket is located at the corner of Route 302 and Route 117, where the fictional Federal Foods Company is located.

Cujo (1981)
Set primarily in fictional Castle Rock. A two-hundred-pound Saint Bernard named Cujo goes from being the lovable pet of a dysfunctional family to a foaming-at-the-mouth killer. A supporting character lives in Bridgton, and a character purchases toy trucks from a fictional Bridgton department store.

King began writing *Cujo* while he was living in Bridgton. The story goes he took his motorcycle to a mechanic who worked out of an auto shop across the road from his rural farmhouse. When he got there, he saw an enormous Saint Bernard come out of the garage and walk toward him, growling.

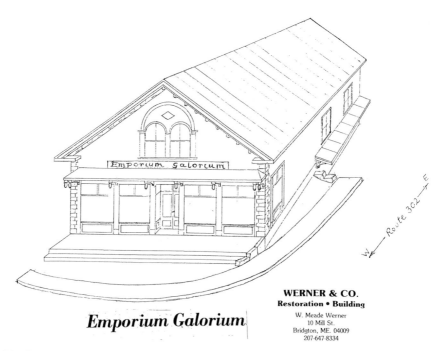

WERNER & CO.
Restoration • Building
W. Meade Werner
10 Mill St.
Bridgton, ME. 04009
207-647-8334

Emporium Galorium

The Emporium was part of a nineteenth-century opera house. When demolished in 1988 as part of Bridgton's revitalization program, it was being used as an antiques shop. *Courtesy of the Bridgton Historical Society.*

"THE SUN DOG," IN KING'S COLLECTION *FOUR PAST MIDNIGHT* (1990)
The story introduces readers to Reginald "Pop" Merrill, the patriarch of the fictional Merrill clan in Castle Rock and a "homespun Mr. Fixit" who runs a junk shop on the town's Main Street called the Emporium Galorium. When a young boy receives a Polaroid instant camera for his birthday and it doesn't work quite right, the boy and his father take it to Merrill to check out. Things sort of "escalate" from there. The real-life inspiration for Merrill's shop was an antique shop called the Emporium that was torn down in 1988 so adjustments could be made to Route 302.

BAG OF BONES (1998)
In mid-December 1977, the Kings bought a home in the lakeside town of Lovell, a half-hour drive from Bridgton. Lovell is the inspiration for the fictional unorganized territory of TR-90, where a large part of King's novel *Bag of Bones* takes place. Kezar Lake, which is partially in Lovell, is the inspiration for fictional Dark Score Lake, which also features in the novel.

Rosie's Village Store (open 2001–21) in Lovell is the inspiration for a location in King's novel *Bag of Bones*. *Photo by author.*

Rosie's Village Store (open 2001–21) in Lovell is the inspiration for the Village Cafe where King's fictional Buddy Jellison is the best fry cook in western Maine. Their chocolate frappes were the richest, creamiest and frothiest.

Under the Dome (2009)

King has said Bridgton is the model for Chester's Mill, a small Maine town suddenly trapped by an invisible force field. When it comes to setting and characters, he took the adage "write about what you know" to heart when writing this novel.

King borrowed the surname for one of the story's primary antagonists, Big Jim Rennie, a used car dealer and the town's corrupt second selectman, from Renys—a chain of department stores located throughout the state of Maine. The Renys in Bridgton is across from Bridgton Books, where King is known to go in and sign books and put them back on the shelf. When interviewed by the *Bridgton News* in 2013, King emphasized the character is not, however, based on anybody from town.

The former Bridgton jail in the basement of the red brick building across from the Magic Lantern is the inspiration for the jail in the novel. Judith Oberg of Oberg Insurance and Real Estate Agency, which currently owns the building, gave me a tour. It was constructed in 1907 to house the Bridgton Savings Bank, but by 1965 the town was using it to house the town office on the main floor, the courthouse on the second floor and the police station in the basement. Next to the tiny former office of the police chief—

The Bridgton location of Reny's, a chain of department stores located throughout Maine. Photo taken sometime in the early 1960s. *Courtesy of the Bridgton Historical Society.*

Cells in the old basement jail in Bridgton. Inspired location in the novel *Under the Dome*. Photo by author.

described as closet size in the book—are two holding cells with wooden benches and iron doors complete with slots to pass through food trays. On the low-hung ceiling, there is writing running along the exposed pipes. King visited the old cells when researching the book.

Eula Shorey, longtime publisher of the *Bridgton News*, a weekly paper serving western Maine since 1870, was King's inspiration for the character Julia Shumway, the editor-publisher of the local paper, the *Chester's Mill Democrat*. Mike Davis says Shorey was friends with King and a real firecracker who knew where all the bodies were buried in town.

What is not certain is how much King, a prolific researcher, knows about the burning of the nearby town of Brownfield in 1947 and how much, if at all, that inspired *Under the Dome*.

The Fire Under the Dome—SPOILER WARNING

In the final part of the novel, Chester's Mill burns. A character mentions Bar Harbor burning back in 1947. This is a reference to the forest fires that burned along the coast of Maine that year.

Could real-life events in Maine's history have inspired the ending of *Under the Dome*? Mike thinks maybe the town of Brownfield, nearly all of which burned, might have.

Brownfield doesn't directly touch Bridgton but borders Fryeburg and Denmark, both of which do. Mike says only a handful of houses in Brownfield survived the fire there in 1947.

In her book *Wildfire Loose: The Week Maine Burned*, author Joyce Butler writes of a fire warden stationed in the lookout tower on Pleasant Mountain (located in Bridgton and Denmark), who was watching. He saw something like a hand closing on a ball when the fire leaped over the town and then closed around it.

"That line stuck with me when folklorist Jo Radner mentioned it during a talk about Brownfield and Fryeburg's history as the great hand that's come to crush the town and how the people watching from the other towns and from the fire tower just know there's nothing they can do," Mike shares.

Mike attended Fryeburg Academy in Fryeburg for high school. During part of that time, he lived in Brownfield and learned a lot about the history of both towns—including some unwritten history.

Old-timers you'd see hanging around the diner or working at the public works—many of those families go back to the families that lived there

A common sight—a logging truck on Route 302 in Bridgton. *Photo by author.*

and survived the fire. There's not the best feeling at all between some of Brownfield's old-timers and the fire department there and the fire department in Fryeburg. That's because, as I understand it, when Brownfield was burning a lot of towns went to Brownfield's aid. Fryeburg, the next town over, it's not that they didn't help, but their efforts were primarily with setting up firebreaks and sandbagging walls and getting the tankers and all the water out to hold the line so it didn't burn Fryeburg too.

The idea of this man-made line cutting off one small Maine town from another. How the Fryeburg Fire Department set up a perimeter to try and enclose the fire in Brownfield strikes me as very Under the Dome.

As noted earlier in this book, King is very intentional. The chances of him mentioning the fire in 1947 and knowing as much history as he does about Maine does not feel coincidental.

11/22/63 (2011)

Jake Epping, the main protagonist of the novel, is a high school English teacher from Lisbon Falls, Maine, who travels back in time to try to prevent the assassination of President Kennedy. He makes a side trip to Derry (another of King's fictional towns) and sees a fallen chimney at the old ironworks. Inside he sees a heap of gnawed bones and something crawling around. He has a really bad feeling and hurries away. It's presumed by readers what Epping encounters was Pennywise, the monster clown from King's 1986 novel *IT*.

Mike says the mills in town would have been derelict by the time King started spending time in Bridgton and that he would have seen a big brick smokestack lying on its side. Was that his inspiration for the scene? It's possible. King has a keen memory for details, and it's been established he was likely in the area while writing the book.

GARY GOMES—BARBER

In between his haircut appointments, I had the opportunity to talk with Gary Gomes, the Barber of Bridgton, and for our purposes, King's Maine barber. He and his wife (and longtime business partner), Jane, are easy to talk to, and Gary especially is a natural storyteller. "Gift for the Gab" is what Stephen calls it, he tells me.

Gary was born in 1959 and grew up in Barnstable County in Massachusetts. Bridgton reminds him of Barnstable in the 1960s and 1970s with all the longtime family-owned businesses. Part of the reason they moved to the Bridgton area around 2010 was because Jane's aging parents lived in a neighboring town. He's had his shop at 22 Main Street in Bridgton since 2017.

The fella who was cutting my hair was the reason why I started. I saw that he only went to school for seven months, he owned his house, he had a nice car, he had a motorcycle. He was very busy all the time, and had a nice place to work. You're inside when it's hot, dry when it's raining, warm when it's cold. It didn't look like a bad deal.

After high school graduation, Gary registered for the seven-month program at the Massachusetts School of Barbering and graduated in 1978. He learned about hair styles and hygiene— how to keep his workspace and

Gary Gomes, the Barber of Bridgton. He cuts Stephen King's hair when he's in town. *Photo by author.*

tools clean and sharp, how to stop the bleeding (Styptic powder and a cold compress). Just enough, he says, to pass the state's exam.

The school (it closed in 1988) was located on Washington Street in the Combat Zone, an area of downtown Boston known for its X-rated movie theaters, strip clubs and adult bookstores. And it was under an elevated section of the Orange Line, a part of the Massachusetts Bay Transportation Authority's subway line. "So, it was like in the movies," Gary shares. "If you were in the classroom and your instructor was talking and the train went by, he had to stop because you couldn't hear him because of the subway going by."

Next door to the school was a pawn shop he says was rumored to be owned by the organized crime boss Whitey Bulger. "I don't know if I ever saw Whitey Bulger or not, but I saw every color combination of the Lincoln Mark VII pull up in front of the pawn shop," Gary shares.

Gary says Stephen King saw an article about him that mentioned he'd gone to barber school. "He remembered his mother taking him to the one in Lewiston when he was young," Gary shares. "So, that was his intrigue. That's how we met."

Every time King comes in, Gary says, he asks him for another story about the barber school.

> *This last time I told him about the leaker. He was so drunk he leaked whenever he'd get in the chair and have a shave. I was the student, so it's hey kid go get the mop. And he's passed out.*

The Bowling Alley and the Barber of C'Ville

After graduating, Gary shares, it took him a couple of years to really develop his skills and gain confidence cutting hair. He started off with a guy named Roger Taggart who ran his own shop called the Jolly Roger in North Eastham, Massachusetts. "I'd say he was probably the best mentor I've had in the profession," Gary says.

In Barnstable County, he found a job with a barbershop in a bowling alley for a few months. Then, unable to find a barbering shop, he became a "Jack of all trades" working multiple odd jobs. By the early eighties, he was back cutting hair, this time at a barbershop next to an auto body shop. When he left there, he started his own business in Centerville and eventually became known as "the barber of C'Ville." "Centerville was called C'Ville, so he became the barber of C'Ville, like the opera only not spelled that way," Jane explains.

Trends

When asked about hair trends, he says it's the same haircut through the years, just with a different name.

> *A mullet is still a mullet; a fade is really a regular men's tapered haircut. High and tight, that's all it is. Or an Ivy Leaguer that's what they called it in the 1960s and '70s and now they call it a fade.*

The first mullet he did was in 1985. When asked how he could remember the exact year, he says it was because Ray Bourque of the Boston Bruins had a mullet. All it takes is one athlete or one movie star to inspire a trend, he explains.

"The same year, *Commando* starring Arnold Schwarzenegger came out," Jane recalls. "He had a version of the flat top—men have shaved head hair flat on top—well he had a longer version. So, we called it the Commando and every kid wanted one [she laughs]. Some parents said well do a real short flat top. Some kids got the longer look."

Customer Appreciation

Gary and Jane say they love their clients from Massachusetts. "We had them for thirty-five years," Janes shares. "Gary gave haircuts to kids and then their kids." Gary has even been known to go to a longtime client's nursing home to cut their hair.

Some of the perks of getting your hair cut by Gary—aside from his stories—he has capes! King's cape has *Shawshank* written on it. There is also a stock of Atomic Fireballs cinnamon-flavored candies, Dum-Dum lollipops and King's favorite Hostess Twinkies snack cakes.

———

EMILY C. GOODNOW—REVEREND

Love is the primary language spoken by Reverend Emily C. Goodnow, the senior pastor at First Congregational Church of Bridgton since 2016. Which makes sense, because she grew up surrounded by love. "It was profound to be so well loved by a community," she says of her youthful days at the United Church of Christ Congregation in Dover, New Hampshire. "They saw me, they got me, they cared for me, they cared for my family. It was really beautiful."

Reverend Goodnow cannot remember a time when she didn't want to be a pastor. "Like I don't remember when I first loved chocolate or when I first knew I loved to hike, I don't remember when I wanted to be a pastor," she tells me.

"The church I grew up at had a red carpet in the sanctuary and my earliest memories are that the carpet felt like home and sanctuary in both of the best senses of those words," the reverend recalls. "I can remember being five maybe and standing with the Sunday school and singing. Our teacher in front of us mouthing the words. And just looking around and feeling joy and safe and loved and happy with my friends who felt like family and all these adults who I knew loved me."

The Methodist Church in West Durham was a substantial part of King's life growing up during the late 1950s and early 1960s. Charles Huff preached the Sunday sermons during that time. In his speech "Huffy" from 1984, which he gave in that little old church, King describes with great affection Mr. Huff. A man who stood about five foot five inches, had intelligent blue eyes and an infectious sense of humor. He favored blue suits and black ties and always wore his Methodist pin. King recalls his unwavering commitment to his God and church and his love of small congregations.

Meeting Reverend Goodnow, she smiles big, laughs hard and the caring just gushes out of her. She, like King's Mr. Huff, is important to her congregation and community.

A Life in Technicolor

While at Yale Divinity School, where she received her master of divinity degree, she interned at a church. She says it felt like she did growing up, that she was home.

> *When I was first articulating it, I would use that scene in the film* The Wizard of Oz *when Dorothy wakes up and she's in color for the first time. I had that feeling. Not that life was black and white in any morose way, but that's life and this is life. When I'm in church, when I'm in community, when I'm invited into pastoral roles, that feels like where things come alive. Where I am my better self. Where life is more joyful.*

In 2013, she was ordained in the United Church of Christ in Dover.

Church's Role in the Community

Founded in 1784, the original home of the church was at 121 Main Street where the Rufus Porter Museum of Art and Ingenuity is located. The white-steepled building at 33 High Street was built in 1871. An addition was built in the 1960s. It is one of eleven churches in Bridgton. The congregation currently numbers 185.

"I hope we are a spiritual refuge where what matters here is we come together around the table and around Christ's teaching," she says. "The dogma and the details don't matter quite as much. I hope we are a community center where people can connect and get to know each other and get woven into each other's lives. And I hope, and I know, this church really is a space of care for our neighbors."

In 2022, the church gave gifts amounting to $19,218.32 to help support members of their congregation by buying heating oil, paying electric bills, purchasing wood, defraying funeral costs, funding medical needs and supporting people recovering from house fires.

We don't just pay the bill; we meet the person—I meet with them—or I meet with them with our leaders and we talk to them about what's going on and we find ways that we can collaborate and care. There are a lot of people as you know who are living on the margins in rural Maine and it looks different—in Portland people stand on the street corners—and in rural Maine people quietly suffer until it's an emergency in their homes, which are not insulated or not safe. Then they call, and we have the true honor and privilege of helping when we can.

Reverend Goodnow says there are members of the congregation who will show up to do everything from building a wheelchair ramp for someone coming home from the hospital to helping winterize a congregation member's home. Reverend Goodnow shares it's not because people write checks for $7,000, it's because they give $5 and $10 here and there.

Stephen King-y Happenings

"In an old church we have a bunch of people who won't come here at night," Reverend Goodnow tells me. "Which is actually very Stephen King-y because things happen in the building. Lights come on and off. There are sounds."

She says people have stories about seeing things.

I used to come early in the mornings on Sundays before I was a parent to go through worship and get myself centered and grounded. We had lost one of our matriarchs. Her name was Ruth, and she was a legend, a force of life. Gentle and wise and strong and funny and all the things. She passed in one of those great stories where the fire alarm in the hospital rang thirty seconds after she passed and for no reason that was known to this world.

After she passed when I would come into the sanctuary all the lights would be off—and this only happened one time—and I'd be talking out loud to myself as is my manner and one of the sconces on the wall would just come on as I was wondering a certain thing. I ended up going with the thing and it was the right thing.

Then, more frequently the lights would all be on and the same sconce would go off. I started to connect it with Ruth and I started to talk out loud to her and say oh Ruth what do you think we should do *and in an unexplainable almost uncomfortable frequency the light would flicker as what felt like an answer.*

The engineers in the church family tell me it's old wiring in the sanctuary, but I believe in my bones that Ruth was communicating at least for a season. And it was also a season when I was needing particular guidance about how to navigate leadership here.

Reverend Goodnow has not read much of King's work but likens what she has to good campfire stories. Rarely, however, she says in real life are the kinds of supernatural or unexplainable encounters he bases stories on scary. In fact, she says to me she feels the experiences are often quite peaceful—like a connection or gift.

ANNA BUTTER AND JEFFREY FREY— CONGREGATION MEMBERS

Lawnmower Story

Growing up in Connecticut, Jeffrey Frey gravitated toward hands-on engineering challenges. He was committed to learning how different systems work. One summer vacation when he was six years old, he was bored and looking for something to do when the family's lawn mower caught his eye and he spent the day taking it apart.

I did it like an illustrated drawing. The wheels were out, the engine components laid out. My father—who was an engineer himself—came home and parked the car and as soon as he opened the car door, I flipped open the garage door. He sat his briefcase on the ground and said "what have you done" and I said "I took this thing apart" and he said "I can't believe you did that you know I can't just go about replacing things because you're curious about how something works" and I told him "I'm going to be put it back together again." He said, "There's no way you can put that thing back together again," so I went to my room chastened.

Jeffrey says his father went off to work the next day and he spent the whole day working on the lawn mower.

So, my father comes home and same thing: garage door opened up and I just started the mower right up and it ran like a clock and he was like what kid of mine could do this. After that, he and I used to go to the dump because there really was a dump back then and I could come home with anything I wanted that would fit in the station wagon. I brought home dishwashers, washing machines, clothes dryers. I started making things out of the sheet metal. Cutting up pieces of it.

Anna then shares that when Jeffrey got a little bit older but still didn't have a driver's license he started buying and fixing up and selling used Volkswagen Beetles.

Save Our Sanctuary: Firm Our Foundation

Jeffrey was the contractor in charge of the church's massive renovation in 2005, which included replacing the crumbling 1800s foundation. That same year, he and his wife, Anna Butter, who both describe themselves as lapsed Catholics, joined the congregation.

Since then, he has been the facilities manager for the church. Over the years, one could say—and Reverend Goodnow does—he and the building have gotten to know each other. Jeffrey explains, "Sometimes this place talks to me related to weather, like when it's particularly cold out." "He'll say, I'm going to go check on the church," Anna says in regards to Jeffrey's sort of sixth sense about the building. He'll arrive when something has just broken and the pipes are minutes from freezing.

Church Potlucks and Stirring with a Canoe Paddle

Jeffrey loves to cook, and when he does, he figures why make one serving when he can make three. One day he made about five gallons of soup and started calling people to see if he could drop some off.

Jeffrey learned to cook at Boy Scouts of America camps on the shores of Lake of Isles in Connecticut. His father was a Scoutmaster, so he and his brother both joined. When his older brother went to interview for a summer camp counselor position, he asked to tag along. He says he was sitting in a chair in the hall while his brother was being interviewed and some "executive type" came up and asked him what he was doing there. Jeffrey told him his brother was interviewing and the man suggested when he was older also working for a camp.

That summer after camp started, they were short-staffed in the kitchen and called Jeffrey to see if he was interested in a job. "I had to tell everybody that I was fifteen years old, and I did not look anywhere near fifteen," he recalls. He had to order special chef whites because of how small he was.

Jeffrey helped cook for nearly 750 people. At one camp, he tells me, the chef baked everything from scratch. "If you had French toast on the menu for the next day you made bread the day before," he says. "At least fifty or sixty loaves of bread. Spaghetti sauce was in a pot that was this big around [he expands his arms] and so tall I would stand on metal milk cages on top of the stove with a canoe paddle stirring it."

Jeffrey loved the experience so much he ended up working at the camps during all his high school summers.

AARON DERR, SENIOR EDITOR of the *Boy Scouts of America Magazine*, documented King's Boy Scouts references in his stories. Following are a few:

SALEM'S LOT
Multiple Scouting references, including mentions of Cub Scouts and a Scout hatchet; one character tells another, "You were never a Boy Scout. I, however, always come prepared."

THE DEAD ZONE
One character learned to use a "Silva compass when he had been in the Scouts"; a later passage mentions "Boy Scouts winning merit badges on The Great Hike of Life."

PET SEMATARY
A character "hadn't held a compass in his hand since Boy Scouts, twenty years before."

IT
One character "believed in the Boy Scout motto," a poster invites families to "JOIN THE SCOUTING EXPERIENCE," mentions of "Scout campouts" and "Boy Scout shorts"; Scouts march in the Derry parade.

11/22/63
A character from the present day preparing to time-travel back to the late 1950s is told not to bring a backpack because, "Where you're going, nobody wears backpacks except Boy Scouts, and they only wear them when they're going on hikes and Camporees"; a later reference mentions a troop of Boy Scouts tending a bonfire with their Scoutmaster.

———

8
FAIR TOWN
FRYEBURG

I n Fryeburg, the best place to eat in early October is Maine's Blue Ribbon
Classic Agricultural Fair at 1154 Main Street. It is the final fair of the
season in Maine, and it's a pretty big deal.

About 3,400 people live in the town of Fryeburg, and during one week
in early October over 220,000 more make the trip there from around New
England. They are pig farmers, woodworkers, pizza makers, off-duty police
officers, a family of fudge makers, kindergarten teachers, junior varsity
baseball players and sixth-generation Christmas tree farmers. They come to
eat candy apples, exhibit livestock, watch sheepdogs compete, judge a skillet
throwing contest, get spun around really fast on a brightly colored ride, win
a blue ribbon, play bingo, check out farm equipment and, in Stephen King's
case, ingest a sausage sandwich covered in grilled onions and peppers.

The Fryeburg Fair, one of the largest in New England, opened in 1851. It
began when a few farmers and shopkeepers got together for a day to highlight
their wares and recognize the importance of agriculture in their community.
Today the fair is an eight-day event and its home 185-acre fairgrounds with
over one hundred permanent structures. In 2022, the fair hired a new ride
vendor, Dreamland Amusements, and for the first time fairgoers could pay
for rides with a credit card. The fair's foundation remains agricultural and is
still 100 percent volunteer run.

With over a century and a half of history under its belt, the fair has
seen generations of families—attendees and vendors—grow up around the
Midway. Grandparents who attended as children bring their grandchildren,

The Fryeburg Fair has blue ribbon–quality concessions from cotton candy and whoopie pies to falafels and Italian sausages with peppers and onions. *Photo by author.*

sharing stories and creating memories. There is something about seeing this in person that transcends an already fun day at the fair—almost as if observing a promise that each successive generation has the responsibility of continuing the tradition.

In the Books

King has been attending the fair since at least the mid-1970s, when he lived in nearby Bridgton, and has incorporated what appears to be a real passion for it into several of his stories. The first mention of the fair I could find is in his 1979 novel *The Dead Zone.* A character who grew up in South Paris is mentioned as having attended the big fair in Fryeburg.

In his novel *IT,* a group of kids who call themselves the "Losers Club" take on the horror show that is "Pennywise the Dancing Clown" in King's fictional town of Derry, Maine, in 1958 and 1985. The primary antagonist knows how to trick his youthful victims into trusting it so it can attack. Prior to terrorizing Stanley Uris, an eleven-year-old boy who is a member of the Losers Club in 1958, it lures him in with the sounds and smells of a country fair. Presumably, King is using the Fryeburg Fair and possibly the Topsham Fair—which he might have attended when growing up in Durham—as his primary inspiration.

The Fryeburg Fair is a classic agricultural fair. The first fair was held in 1851. Mentioned in several of King's stories. *Photo by author.*

In *The Tommyknockers*, the primary character Jim Gardener recalls going to the fair as a ten-year-old and going through the Mirror Maze.

In *Bag of Bones*, the primary protagonist is Mike Noonan, a recently widowed novelist. Noonan spends a summer at the couple's haunted lakeside house in western Maine. At one point, he experiences an early twentieth-century Fryeburg Fair: the merry-go-round, a high striker (a manly man bangs the bell at the top of a tower), a shooting gallery, blue ribbon cows, fried dough, grilled onions and peppers, cotton candy, manure and hay.

RACHEL ANDREWS DAMON AND BARBARA HILL—FAIR ORGANIZERS

In the mid-1960s, Rachel Andrews Damon and Barbara Hill were young farm girls in Fryeburg building treehouses, playing ball in neighbors' fields and attending Girl Scout meetings.

145

"Back then we only got one television channel, biking was a big thing and it was a pretty darn good time," Rachel shares. "You could play an entire baseball game in the road and there wouldn't be a car coming by."

Barbara recalls riding her bicycle on field roads and how a lot of the kids wanted to play ball at one family's house because they had a big field. "I would go down there and I remember Vonette, the mother, calling my mother and saying, 'Peggy I'm sending her home now I've had enough,' and out the door I'd go," she says.

Rachel shares that while she felt her rural childhood was idyllic, she dreamed of seeing the bright lights of New York City. "I had this tiny transistor radio that if I got in a certain place in the house I could hear stations from New York City, which I thought was the biggest thing in the world," Rachel says.

There's a story that Rachel's grandfather Phil Andrews, who owned North Fryeburg's Riverside Farm, at one time the largest dairy farm in Maine, paid the doctor in maple syrup for delivering her father. In 1969, around the time Rachel was a preteen, her father left the family's farming business and went to work for the Oxford County Sheriff's Department and became the chief deputy sheriff.

Crime in the Countryside

Curious about her unique outlook as the daughter of a member of rural law enforcement, and because one of King's primary themes is violent crime in small towns, I ask Rachel her thoughts regarding how small towns have been stereotyped as the reflection of innocence.

I don't want to say Fryeburg was innocent, because bad things happened. But you didn't really talk about it or analyze it like you do now. If someone went to the store and you saw them buying a six-pack of beer, that was really something to run home and tell your mother. I just think looking back there's a lot of stuff people just didn't talk about. Child abuse, that kind of thing. Abuse on spouses. There was a lot of poverty and not a lot of education. It was a fallout from those kinds of things. I'm just talking about an atmosphere that was more secretive than today.

Barbara adds that parents never talked in front of their kids. It just wasn't done, she tells me.

A History & Guide

Rachel says she would sit on the stairs when her father came home from work so she could listen to what he told her mother about his day. She explains she wanted to know, but she also didn't. "It's like it's your childhood and you're out having fun and things are good and flowers are growing and you hear some story that derails you," she shares. "But that's the growing up part."

To protect her daughter, without talking about why she felt she needed protecting, Rachel's mother would center social activities at their house. "You wouldn't even know she was keeping an eye on us, but it was just more comfortable and I did the same thing with my kids," she says. "If they'd say, can I go spend the night at someone's house, I'd say no but why don't you have them spend the night here and bring this one too. So, it would make it more attractive, and we had a lot of kids at our house."

For the Love of the Fair

Another way Rachel's parents kept her busy and presumably in sight was getting her and her siblings involved in the organizing of the fair. It was, after all, something generations of her family had been involved in. Her grandfather and an uncle were past presidents of the fair. "I have missed two in my life, and I'm sixty-four," she says.

Rachel started working at the fair when she was twelve, and she thought it was the coolest thing in the world. "My brother and I paged people," she shares of the pre-cellphone era. "People would come up and say really stupid names like page Benjamin Dover. You can call him Ben. So, we'd be like Ben Dover ["bend over"], ha ha. We'd have a line of one hundred people waiting to page someone to go to the car, to go to the Ferris wheel, to go to the main gate. That was my first interworking at the fair and we just loved it, and we've loved the fair all our lives."

When asked what she loves most about the fair, Rachel says, "The colors, the smells, the taste, the feel of that time of year." And the French fries she loves because they're made with Maine potatoes. She tells me everyone just seems like they're having a really good time and taking it all in. As part of her job as publicist for the fair, she takes photos for social media and loves photographing the farmers and people who work the rides. She shares that she wonders what their life is like.

Barbara enjoys the food—especially the French fries. She points out there are bottles of vinegar at every stand. Also sausage sandwiches, and always

147

from Mr. and Mrs. Sausage—which also happens to be King's go-to food vendor when he attends the fair.

When Barbara moved back to the area from New York in 2010 after twenty years, the first thing she did was go with her mother to buy herself a Lifetime Fryeburg Fair Pass. "Those first few years I was back I came out to the fair every single day," she shares. "Sometimes I came out for breakfast to see the sights, [listen to] the sounds. All those tactile things."

Growing up, Barbara attended the fair every year.

It was always the same. We parked out in an area that's covered with vendors now. You drove in and parked your car and angled any way you wanted and what not. My mother always packed a picnic basket loaded with tuna fish sandwiches, potato chips and pickles. And again, it was very much like home, you got to the fair and here's your money and go have a good time. My father would go to the pulling ring. We just wandered around. It was OK to do that. My mother eventually tired of the pulling ring, and she loved playing Beano—Bingo played with beans. She dragged me along to play with her and I loved that. We would laugh! The only ride she would go on was the Tilt-a-Whirl and as a result of that I loved it, because we would have a good time and laugh doing that. You were seated in these half-open carriages, and they would spin around on a separate disc and the disc would go around and you could lean to get them spinning fast.

Barbara says she also enjoyed the carnival games and winning small stuffed animals.

Let's Talk about Stephen King

Both Barbara and Rachel read King. "Everybody who's read his books can see themselves in them in some way," Rachel shares. "People love Stephen King. I love Stephen King." She thinks one of the things King likes to do at the fair, aside from eating a sausage sandwich, is people watch. "To sit down with your Diet Coke and fries and just watch people is great," she tells me. "I can't imagine that he doesn't get a whole lot of material from watching people here."

King's novel *Dolores Claiborne* is one of Rachel's favorite books. The titular character is a plain-spoken, middle-aged widowed mother living on an imaginary Maine island who is accused of murdering her wealthy elderly employer.

> *When I first read it, I said who the hell is this Stephen King guy. He's probably just another one of those people who thinks they're a Mainer. And I went into it with this really shitty attitude, and then I'm reading it and I'm like and he's going to write about women. So, I didn't really think that this person was viable in the beginning. By the time I got done with that book, (a) it is one of my favorite books ever and (b) I could not believe what a handle he had on Maine and then I could not believe that a man could write that well about women.*
>
> *I don't think he's demeaning to Mainers. I think he's very real, which is what Mainers really, really appreciate. I once maybe thirty years ago went to a Walden's Books in the mall in North Conway and they had an entire section for Stephen King. So, I went in there, and I never thought the people in there were that friendly, and then one day I said, you know, "What is your favorite Stephen King book?" because I have a journalistic sense of things as well. It then became the entire store. Maybe eight people weighing in on Stephen King and his writing. It was probably one of the greatest conversations I've ever had with strangers. Everybody loves him.*

"Oh, and of course I love *Bag of Bones*," she says, adding that she's positive the owner of Thurston's Garage in neighboring Lovell, Maine, inspired a supporting character in the book. "Ever since reading that book years ago whenever, I drive by that garage I think of Stephen King," she shares.

*In March 2023, after fifty-five years of business, the family who owned the automotive shop Rachel refers to sold it.

DANA LEVASSEUR—FAIR FOOD VENDOR

The week leading up to Memorial Day weekend, Dana Levasseur serves up sausage sandwiches out of his food truck in the parking lot of the information center on Route 2 in Rumford, Maine. From there he makes stops at multiple fairs across Maine before arriving at the Fryeburg Fair in October. He's not done until after the fair, when he opens back up in Rumford for a weekday or weekend here and there. Then it's off to the Caribbean on a cruise or two for a much-needed and well-deserved break.

At the Fryeburg Fair, and likely at all his stops, his sandwiches have devotees—the Kings included. What sets them apart, he says, is his tomato sauce. "It brings out the flavor of the sausage," he explains.

Dana grew up in Auburn, Maine. He got into the carnival business while in high school through friends whose parents traveled with the carnival. His first full-time job was the day after graduation in 1993.

"I left Auburn, Maine, and went to Auburn, Massachusetts, to work for a couple who owned two rides and a fried dough stand, 'Jensen's Fried Dough,'" Dana says. He worked for them off and on for several years.

In the late nineties, they traveled with Fiesta Shows—a New England–based traveling amusement provider—and that's where Dana met the original Mr. & Mrs. Sausage, Skip and Ada Brawn. He worked for them in 1999. Skip passed away in 2000, and his son took over. Dana helped him out at fairs on the weekends, as he'd taken a full-time position at a catalogue printer in Lisbon, Maine. In 2009, Lee asked him to purchase the business, and in 2010, Dana officially took over.

"I had been around so long that all the customers and everyone thought I was family," he shares. "Most of the customers are regulars. I can't remember all their names, but I remember their faces and can remember how they want their sandwiches."

A Day at the Fair

At the Fryeburg Fair, Dana's day starts around 6:30 a.m. with the walk over to the stand. Around 7:00 a.m., the grills get turned on, and the cooking for the day starts. The sausage takes around forty-five minutes to cook. The onions and bell peppers are cooked on a separate grill with vegetable oil, salt, pepper and garlic. In the bottom of the roll, he usually puts a little of that special tomato sauce before the sausage and peppers and onions.

We judge how busy of a day it will be according the line at the jumbo donuts next to us. The longer the line, the busier it will be for us at lunchtime. Meanwhile, while everyone is in line for donuts they are forced to take in the aroma of sausage, onions, peppers and garlic. Lunchtime is the busy part of the day for us. Around three in the afternoon it slows

Stephen King purchasing a sandwich from Mr. and Mrs. Sausage, a popular vendor at the Fryeburg Fair. *Courtesy of Dana Levasseur of Mr. and Mrs. Sausage.*

down so we can get cleaned up from the mess we made during lunch rush. And also start peeling and slicing onions for the next day. At nine it's closing time and shower time.

He estimates he goes through over 1,000 pounds of sausage and around 1,300 pounds of onions for the fair. "That's a lot of crying," he says.

He thinks the Kings come the same day every year but won't say which day so they are not harassed. "When people come up to the counter and ask, 'Is Stephen still here,' we reply with 'Yeah, we hobbled him, he's in the prep tent peeling onions for us.'"

———

9
WOOD SPLITTERS
BACK TO SCHOOL: ORONO

On a spring day in 1970, a ream of heavy green paper was propelled into the annals of literary history. Up until this day, the paper had a pretty mundane future in store—that of being used to print timecards for employees of the Raymond H. Fogler Library at the University of Maine at Orono. However, as luck would have it, a library director had requested the cleaning up and clearing out of a closet. Reams of blue paper and green paper were found. Rather than see them go to waste, this director called the work studies students over and asked if any of them would like some of the colored paper. Among the crowd of students was Stephen King. He went on to use that green paper to print a manuscript of *The Dark Tower: The Gunslinger*, the first volume in King's Dark Tower series.

Desiree Butterfield-Nagy, an obliging archivist in Fogler's Special Collections Department, shared this story. She says she believed the rumor because up until recently the library had huge stocks of the blue and green paper that employees were still using for their timecards.

This Is Maine, Baby. Not Berkeley

King attended the University of Maine between 1966 and 1970. During that time, Orono didn't see the storm of antiwar protests like those taking place on college campuses in California and New York. There were marches in opposition to the war in Vietnam and candle-lit services, but otherwise student life remained largely consistent with what it had been before.

University of Maine president Winthrop C. Libby addressing students in 1970. Stephen King can be seen third from left (in glasses and collared short-sleeved shirt) sitting behind him. *Photograph courtesy of Special Collections, Raymond H. Fogler Library, University of Maine, Orono, Maine.*

Students attended environmental awareness activities, horror film festivals, ice races on nearby Pushaw Lake, fraternity parties and baseball games and complained about tuition increases. They wore bell-bottom pants and black cowboy boots. They used words like *groovy, dig it* and *far out.*

The UMaine campus, which was founded in 1865, is about one mile from downtown Orono. The campus is chock full of stunningly beautiful early twentieth-century buildings, a number of which were designated by the National Register of Historic Places in 1978 as a historic district. It is also a haven for outdoor enthusiasts with numerous hiking and biking trails.

The novel-length supernatural coming-of-age tale *Hearts in Atlantis,* in King's collection of the same name, is based on King's first year at UMaine. It's 1966, and the story follows Pete Riley and his freshman classmates at UMaine as they try to maintain their grades to avoid the Vietnam draft while becoming addicted to a card game.

The story is also in the collection *Hearts in Suspension,* a book by King and several of his college classmates about their real-life experiences at UMaine during the Vietnam War era.

Campus Tour

For most of his adult life, Geremy Chubbuck has been accustomed to fixing things. Since 2008, he's been the person in charge of fixing everything on the six-hundred-acre UMaine at Orono campus. He heads up a crew of a couple hundred who mow the lawns, remove the trash, clean the buildings, patch and paint, repair the HVAC systems, change the light bulbs and unclog toilets. His formal title is associate executive director for maintenance and operations at the University of Maine Office of Facilities Management.

"We're the behind-the-scenes folks that make it happen so that folks who are in front of the scenes can do what they need to do," he says.

Geremy graduated from the University of Maine at Orono in 1993 with an engineering degree.

One day in April 2023, he played tour guide for me. First stop, the Folger Library. The building was constructed between 1941 and 1947. With over 3.6 million volumes on its shelves, it is likely one of the busiest academic buildings on campus.

On the second floor, in the high-ceilinged sunlit space known as the Presidents Room, portraits of past university presidents line the walls. This is one of Geremy's favorite spots on campus. The study carrels look inviting, the perfect place to spend a long afternoon reading.

Gannett Hall on the University of Maine campus. King lived here his freshman year. *Photograph courtesy of Special Collections, Raymond H. Fogler Library, University of Maine, Orono, Maine.*

The third floor is the quiet floor and also one of my favorite spots on campus, because it houses the Special Collections department. This is where King's books are stored. As of 2019, however, his papers are no longer there. In the future, the papers are expected to be available on a restricted basis at his former residence in Bangor.

It was in the stacks of the library where King met his future wife, Tabitha Spruce, from nearby Old Town.

We follow up with a quick tour of Memorial Union, the hub for student life and home to the Bear's Den—where *Pet Sematary*'s protagonist Louis Creed has dinner with a colleague. Then on to Gannett Hall, located on the northwest side of the campus, where King lived on the second floor. Based on a photograph of the campus from the 1960s, he would have had a nice view of a grassy quad and a burgeoning athletic facility.

U Maine's Most Famous Alumni

From his sophomore year, King stretched his creative muscles writing the weekly column "King's Garbage Truck" for the university's newspaper, the *Maine Campus*. Column subjects ranged from folk dance performances to film reviews and campus protests. Franco Zeffirelli's film adaptation of Shakespeare's *Romeo and Juliet* warranted a few appearances. Actress Olivia Hussey, who starred in that film, also had a prominent role in the 1990 television adaptation of King's *IT*. The columns are personable, witty and quirky. They are very King-esque, delighting in the grotesque details of university life, defending the working class and obsessing about the genius of scary stories.

During March of his senior year, there was a total solar eclipse. This is when the moon passes between the sun and Earth, casting a shadow on Earth that either fully or partially blocks the sun's light in some areas. This rare astronomical event also occurred on July 20, 1963, when King was nearly six years old. He includes the event in both his novels *Gerald's Game* and *Dolores Claiborne*, both of which feature a 1963 map showing the eclipse path over Maine.

In May 1970, King graduated with a bachelor's degree in English.

Stories that mention or are at least partially set on the University of Maine campus at Orono include the novella *The Body* in King's collection *Different Seasons*, *Hearts in Atlantis* and *Lisey's Story*.

In Honor of Mom

The Nellie Ruth Pillsbury King Memorial Scholarship provides financial assistance to students in good academic standing majoring in English, with a preference for those studying creative writing or literature.

———

DR. MALCOLM L. HUNTER JR.—PROFESSOR EMERITUS OF WILDLIFE ECOLOGY

Long before Dr. Malcolm Hunter was a professor, around the time he might have been pedaling a tricycle, he started saving money to buy a cow. That was when he was three years old, and farming seemed like a good idea. At some point, possibly when young Mackie had graduated to a bicycle, the idea of being a farmer seemed less appealing and he became convinced it was all about being a veterinarian.

Depending on whom you ask, Dr. Hunter is an outdoor enthusiast, biologist, herpetologist, educator, birdwatcher, scuba diver, world traveler, researcher and/or author. His UMaine webpage reads "Professor Emeritus of Wildlife Ecology, Libra Professor of Conservation Biology."

Tasks he has recently crossed off his to-do list: being a regional coordinator for the Maine Bird Atlas project and editing the book *Our Maine: Exploring Its Rich Natural Heritage.*

Dr. Hunter grew up in the Damariscotta, Maine area. Between his undergraduate and faculty years, he has a four-decade association with the University of Maine.

In his spare time, Dr. Hunter is a voracious reader. Also, he maintains a spreadsheet of all the books he has read and rates them on a one to five scale. Of the several hundred he's read, only ten got a five—the best score. Of those ten, two were by King: the novel *11/22/63* and collection *Different Seasons.* There are good storytellers, and there are great ones.

Early Interest in Nature

Family legend has it that my first ten words were mommy, daddy, raccoon, fox, squirrel, *etc. There was a mobile hanging over my crib*

157

with animals. Apparently, I learned all the names at an early age. My parents were proud of the fact that I could say squirrel when I was fourteen months old. It started really young with me.

Dr. Hunter's interest in the natural world began with mammals and then progressed to reptiles and amphibians. His parents supported his interests, supplying him with inexpensive field guides. During his teenage years, his interest expanded to birds when he got a pair of binoculars. When he and his wife began scuba diving, they got into fish. Now they travel all over the world to see fish.

Reginald Roberts

A teacher can have a life-changing effect on a student. For me, it was Paul Belair, ninth-grade history. A teacher who can communicate their passion for the subject they are teaching to the students. Who can offer substantive lessons and help them discover new things. For Dr. Hunter, that was Reginald Roberts.

"I had a truly excellent biology teacher," Dr. Hunter shares. "He was somebody who would take us on field trips to Bowdoin to read the primary literature—not just encyclopedias. I really got into that and decided I wanted to be a high school biology teacher like him."

However, when he figured out university professors got a better deal than high school biology teachers, his trajectory moved up a notch. He aspired to become a university professor, and that's where he ended up.

The Largest Turtle in the World

Dr. Hunter enjoys talking about critters. Right now, he is excited about leatherback turtles, which are occasionally spotted off the coast of Maine. Not in great abundance, he stresses, but they are there and he has personally seen them twice.

He proceeds to share a substantial amount of information with me regarding these mythical-size turtles. I learn they can grow to almost eight feet and weigh up to a ton. They are able to swim in the cold waters of the Gulf of Maine, they eat jellyfish and they are so huge not many things can eat them.

"The leatherback turtle is too large to be vulnerable to most predators, but a few iconic predators have been documented," Dr. Hunter reads from an upcoming book titled *Our Maine: Exploring Its Rich Natural Heritage*, which he edited. "Killer whales and crocodiles by sea, and tigers and jaguars when they come ashore."

Rattlesnakes

One of the reasons I wanted to speak with Dr. Hunter is because he is a snake expert. In May 2022, King spoke with members of *The Losers' Club* podcast, a group of longtime King readers who have been a source of joy for the nerdiest of us King fans since they first started broadcasting in 2017. King told them he'd written a story called "Rattlesnakes." The plot, he said, involves four-year-old twins who fall into a rattlesnake pit. King referred to the short story as a sequel to his novel *Cujo*. In August 2023, King announced on the *Talking Scared* podcast he has a six-hundred-page collection titled *You Like It Darker* coming out in 2024. King fans are hoping "Rattlesnakes" will be included.

In Maine, we have black racers, ringnecks, milk snakes, green snakes and a few other nonvenomous snakes. Common garter snakes are the most common. Rattlesnakes—which are shy, often nocturnal and tend to be in remote areas—used to be found in Maine but were killed off by humans likely by the beginning of the twentieth century.

Dr. Hunter had a case of a potential rattlesnake sighting in the Portland, Maine area.

I happened to get a call, and a woman says, "I understand you know about snakes, and I've caught a rattlesnake." I said, "Where is it?" and she said, "I'm holding it." And I said, "Really—and you can see rattles on the tail of this thing?" And she said, "Yeah." I was half an hour away, so she gave me her address. I drove there. But it wasn't a rattler, it was a milk snake. It might have been trying to imitate a rattlesnake. It was wiggling its tail.

There has been talk about restoring them, but according to Dr. Hunter that's very unlikely to happen.

Truth Stranger than Fiction

Dr. Hunter's wife, Aram Calhoun—a fellow UMaine faculty member—is best known for her work with vernal pools, two key species of which are spotted salamanders and wood frogs. "She makes a big deal of the fact that wood frogs can freeze solid," he says. "It's really quite extraordinary. She's got this great photograph of frozen frogs, and she calls them frogsicles."

He explains most of Maine's amphibians and reptiles find a place to hibernate that's around the freezing temperature by digging deep or going under water. So, it's remarkable the wood frogs are able to tolerate an extraordinary degree of freezing.

A fantastic and short King story is "Rainy Season" in *Nightmares and Dreamscapes*. In the story, a husband and wife rent a house in the fictional town of Willow, Maine. Upon their arrival, some well-worn locals encourage them to head out of town before the rain and come back after it. While that may seem odd and inhospitable, it's actually quite sage advice—at least in Willow. The unlucky duo opts to stay. When the "rain" begins, well, things sure do get interesting—and so do the toads.

JOHN BEAR MITCHELL—NATIVE AMERICAN STORYTELLER

When Stephen King decided to create a cemetery for deceased pets, he did it on top of an ancient Native American burial ground. That was for his 1983 novel *Pet Sematary*. Sixteen years later, he borrowed a mythological evil spirit from Native American folklore for an appearance in his novel *The Girl Who Loved Tom Gordon*.

The Penobscot people have lived in what we now call Maine for thousands of years. The four Indigenous tribes in Maine are the Maliseet, Micmac, Penobscot and Passamaquoddy, known collectively as the Wabanaki, "People of the Dawnland."

John Bear Mitchell is a citizen of the Penobscot Nation and since 2000 has been a teacher at the university. His name in the Wabanaki language is Chacheemouinmahuswon. John points out this is not a translation of his name in English.

John is the University of Maine System Office Native American Waiver and Educational Program Coordinator, the university's Wabanaki Center Outreach and Student Development Coordinator and a lecturer of Wabanaki Studies and Multicultural Studies at the University of Maine in Orono. He grew up on Indian Island, the tribal headquarters of the Penobscot Nation. A bridge links the island and the town of Old Town.

John has told Wabanaki stories on radio shows and podcasts and in theatrical productions. He has also been hired by film and television productions as a cultural consultant. Be sure to look for him in the credits for *Welcome to Derry*, HBO's prequel series about the origins of Pennywise—King's infamous serial killer clown.

Indigenous Knowledge

We were always told by the elders that you introduce yourself—in Passamaquoddy—to the spot you're going to camp, to the river that's going to take you somewhere or any medicines that you might take beforehand. Because in those places our ancestors exist, and they want to recognize you by your family. Who you are. Where you come from. That's how they know if we're related. So, anytime I go somewhere I always introduce myself to the space outside. Anywhere in New England, that was the language that for thousands of years everything heard before Europeans arrived on Penobscot Nation land. Our language was embedded not only into the air, but into the ground.

I recognize that anything that I approach is older than me and that I am to respect it as my elder. The rocks, the rivers, the hills, the land. That's always the way it is. That was something that just became as standard as shaking a hand.

We're traditional people looking for ceremonial protection. When I introduce myself, I hope I am accepted. I ask the grandmothers and grandfathers of the past to protect me. I want to recognize that space almost as a superior.

When we go into the woods, it's like checking into a hotel. You can't just go into a hotel and break down a door and go and utilize the hotel. You have to check in, do the protocol. Make sure you know where things are, where your place is.

Not Your Average Day

On an average day, the drive from Indian Island to Unity takes about one hour. On a snowy day, it's going to take a bit longer. In 1988, John made the trip driving his brother's Honda Civic, which was front-wheel drive and kind of a new thing to him. He was going to talk to an elementary school class and was so nervous he felt sick. John tells me while driving he read and reread the story he was going to share.

He parked his car in front of the school, and as he was walking up to the entrance, he saw all these kids looking out this big bay window at him. It was the beginning of what would turn out to be a very big day.

I was like what the heck, why are they all looking out the window. *I went in and I was guided into the classroom, and it was the classroom where everybody was looking out the window. And the teacher said, "I need to apologize to you. They all ran to the window and I know you noticed them. They made wagers on what color your horse was going to be,"* she said. *"I've been trying to tell them you guys drive cars." And I said* oh my god I'm here for more than just storytelling. I'm here to kind of introduce us in the modern way to these kids.

He told them the story he had practiced, and they loved it and asked him to tell them another. "I told them one I heard my great-grandfather tell," he shares. "That one I had more feeling in, because it was a family story. Then they started asking questions like, "What do your houses look like?" And so, I said *OK this is good."*

Leatherface

John taught a class about Native Americans in films. An art professor from his undergrad days had approached him about doing the class. He says this professor knew he was involved in *Colonial House*, an Emmy-nominated PBS television series about what life looked like in Plymouth Colony in 1628. And he knew John had worked with Gunnar Hansen.

John explains Hansen lived on Mount Desert Island. He was an independent filmmaker who wrote a script for a documentary about the Penobscot River John consulted on. Oh, and his claim to fame was giving life to the horror character called Leatherface in the 1974 movie *The Texas Chain Saw Massacre.*

John was good buddies with Hansen, who was definitely less famous for his documentary work than acting credits including the Strangler in *Hollywood Chainsaw Hookers*.

Gunnar heard about the film audition for Texas Chainsaw *from a former classmate of his. He specifically loved being in B-rated horror movies. Gunnar had made these documentaries, and I was good friends with him. But I didn't know he invented Leatherface. He never talked about it. One time I went down to his home for dinner and he had a friend over—and it was Robert Englund who played the* Nightmare on Elm Street *guy. Yeah, well that guy was sitting there. Little guy and he looked so familiar. And Gunnar says, "This is my friend Bob. Robert, but call him Bob." So, we hung out for a while, and I said, "That guy looks so familiar," and Gunnar was like, "He is best known for playing the supernatural serial killer Freddy Krueger in the franchise* A Nightmare on Elm Street.*"*

Gunnar hated chainsaws. He had the chain taken off of it when filming. He got paid $800 during spring break from graduate school. At the time that was a lot of money. All he had to do was run around with a chainsaw scaring people. But he said, "I didn't want my face on it because it was hokey and corny so I put this mask on and I called myself Leatherface."

He always had a white Volvo station wagon no matter what. Every time an old one would die, he'd get a new one. He had this sticker on the back, "What would Leatherface do?" That's all it said, and otherwise you would never have known. A gentle giant.

King's Inspiration

In King's short story "Drunken Fireworks" from his collection *The Bazaar of Bad Dreams*, two families—one poor and one rich—go toe to toe every Fourth of July competing against each other for who has the biggest, baddest fireworks display.

At one point, the poor family travels to Indian Island to buy fireworks from a big Indian named Howard Gamache. He's described as having feathers tattooed on his cheeks and riding a Harley motorcycle. In real life, Howard Mitchell was John's uncle. He graduated from the Culinary Institute of America and taught at the Johnson and Wales Culinary Institute. John says

Howard used to ride around with King and cook for him occasionally. He says that Howard was six feet, three inches tall, 280 pounds and could keep people away from King if he needed to.

Note, King readers, the Howard Gamache in "Drunken Fireworks" is not related as best I can tell to the Homer Gamache killed by George Stark early on in King's 1989 novel *The Dark Half.*

John says nothing King writes is entirely fiction. He recalls the short story "Herman Wouk Is Still Alive" from King's 2015 collection *The Bazaar of Bad Dreams*. In the story, a woman, a friend and their children are traveling at an excessive speed on the interstate in a rented van. The woman crashes the car, and everyone in the vehicle dies.

John says reading that story, he knows King saw the same real-life accident he drove by in 2004. In that case, a woman driving a rented sport utility full of passengers was going over one hundred miles per hour on the interstate while traveling in the breakdown lane. John explains that King described details of the aftermath not reported in the newspaper.

> *So, I know he attaches place and people. Of course, it's not real in his stories, but if you know, you know when you're reading something. I think he intentionally misdirects. I think he does it to create mystery and mischief and confusion. For those who recognize it around where his head is at. That's why his character development is so intense.*

In an article in the May 11, 2005 edition of the *Lewiston Sun Journal* recalling the accident, there is mention of a sign with "Angels Gather Here" spray-painted on a bedsheet placed among tree trunks near where the site of the real-life accident took place a year earlier. In his story, King describes this exact sign.

King has said he was inspired by a car accident in Parksville, New York, that happened in July 2009. A woman was driving a borrowed minivan full of passengers the wrong way on the highway. Everyone in the vehicle was killed.

10

QUEEN CITY

BANGOR

The decorative two-story red Italianate-style villa with tall, narrow windows on West Broadway, a quiet tree-lined street in Bangor, Maine, is the most photographed attraction in town. Actually, it's probably one of the most photographed in the state. At any given time, a sagging airless red balloon left behind by one of King's fans—a nod to the lead antagonist in King's novel *IT*—can be found tied to the wrought-iron fence. Stephen and Tabitha King are rarely there these days. Still, it attracts a daily stream of King fans. I've been twice.

The house was built around 1855 for William Arnold, a successful livery stable owner. He lived there for only two years before moving to a more modest residence in town. It is believed he ran out of money. Around 1890, a veranda was added, and in 1910, a wrap-around porch replaced the front steps.

In 1971, King began teaching English classes at Hampden Academy, the public high school in Hampden, Maine. He wrote at night and on weekends while living with Tabitha and their daughter, Naomi, in a rented trailer. By 1973, son Joe Hill had come along and a year later so had Doubleday & Company. The publisher accepted Stephen King's novel *Carrie* for publication. On Mother's Day 1974, Doubleday bought the paperback rights for $400,000 ($2,793,394 today). With that, he left teaching, began writing full-time, helped his mother retire and moved his family to nearby Bangor.

Downtown Bangor mural *Bangor Wants You* painted by Annette Dodd, owner of Bangor's Rock & Art Shop. Inspired by the local landmark, a thirty-one-foot Paul Bunyan. *Photo by author.*

After several years of continued success as a writer, Stephen King and his family moved into the nineteenth-century mansion in 1980.

Terry Steel, a blacksmith based in Bridgton, Maine, at the time, made and installed the iconic wrought-iron fence embellished with bats, spiders and a web on its front gates. A Maryland native, Steel had one of the last

Bangor's historic downtown contains a variety of architectural styles dating from the nineteenth century. The city is the inspiration for King's fictional town of Derry. *Photo by author.*

blacksmith shops on Depot Street in Bridgton according to Mike Davis from the Bridgton Historical Society. Mike says historically blacksmiths and carriage people had shops there, and later, characters involved with the railroad lived there.

In 2020, Josh Landry, a chainsaw sculptor, turned a dead ash tree on the Kings' front lawn into a stunning work of art featuring books and animals. The piece was commissioned by Tabitha King.

Although the Kings no longer live there, it is private property and is not open to the public.

In October 2019, the Bangor City Council approved the Kings' plan to turn their home into a writers' retreat and archive. Stephen King posted on social media that the property would welcome up to five writers in residence at a time and that his archives formerly held at the University of Maine at Orono would be accessible for restricted visits by appointment only. He was clear there will not be a museum or any part of the property open to the public. At the time, the Kings believed they would begin operating the retreat in a year or two. The pandemic and who knows what else has delayed those plans.

The Making of Derry

In March 1983, the Bangor Historical Society hosted a fundraiser. The lucky patrons there that night received a program, which included an original essay by King—"A Novelist's Perspective on Bangor." In the essay, King references a novel he is working on that runs 1,200 pages. *IT*, his story about a shape-shifting, child-murdering clown by the name of Pennywise, ran nearly that when published in 1986. Though King does not mention the work by name, it is safe to assume that's the work he is talking about. The essay goes on to provide valuable insight into King's approach to storytelling and place making. King discusses wanting to capture the myths and stories of everyday life in a small American city. How he did this before, but with the small rural town where he grew up—Durham, Maine—in his novel *Salem's Lot*.

A couple people told me that before writing *IT*, King walked all over Bangor learning the history and folklore of the town. He spoke with locals and learned about the missing blueprints for the town's extensive 1930s era sewer system—of note, Pennywise resides in the city's sewer system.

King has said in numerous interviews through the years that Derry is Bangor. Like Castle Rock, it is a place he keeps returning to in his stories. *IT* was the first story that took place in Derry. The most recent was *Gwendy's Final Task*, published in 2022.

Long before the lumber barons got rich off the northern Maine woods and hundreds of sawmills dotted the landscape, the area known as Bangor was the homeland of the Penobscot Nation.

John Bear Mitchell, a citizen of the Penobscot Nation, grew up about a twenty-five-minute drive from Bangor on Indian Island.

I think if you go back to pre-contact time, so before Europeans came here, Bangor was a rallying place for Indigenous people. It was the head of the tidewater. Easy in, easy out. We have stories that go back about Viking contact in that area three thousand years ago. There was a lot of energy in this area. All the time people coming and going. And when you have that there are misdeeds that happen all the time within human existence. Not to say Indigenous people were all good and living in harmony; we had problems. How we know that is we have wampum law and wampum consequence.

Wampum is a belt, and it tells a story. Wampum actually means it's talking. It's a bead made out of purple and white shells. These tubular beads were sewn together in patterns that told stories—whether it was the beginning, middle or end. The symbolism sparks the person who knows how to read its memory and they would know the story.

These belts were our original sort of book. Something we learned from. We have a whole set of wampum belts, and they tell us about the laws we don't break and what the consequence is if we do. And the law is written by the creator and the consequence is carried out by the human on the human. So, we know that we had issues. We know bad people were among us too. Because these are ancient messages up to four thousand years old.

Sometimes energy embeds within the earth and creates physical badness within the land, especially in rock. We have different rocks for different months of our birth. There are different stones for when you were born you are supposed to carry with you in life. But not one of them is granite, because granite holds the energy in our way. We never built our camps or our buildings upon granite, because it was a spiritual energetic rock in a way. Instead, we honored the iron.

If you look at Katahdin Iron Works where he talks about this silo that blew up in IT. *We used red ochre, which is a bleeding of the iron into the soil that forms this clay. That was a highly ceremonial clay for us. We'd dry it and use it on our bodies. We had these burial practices using red ochre to line graves. All along the Penobscot River from the Edington Bend all the way down the Brewer side and on the Bangor side too. Over years and years those burial sites formed these perfectly red circles on the top of the soil. Our burial grounds extended down into the Bangor area in Archaic times. Keep in mind that was only about one thousand years after the tides started. We didn't have tidal water on the coast of Maine except maybe down south. And now it's the head of the tidewater in that area. So, there's all this energy that's in there and you can feel it when you're paddling down in the Kenduskeag Stream. This high cliff rocky energetic area.*

Note, the Katahdin Iron Works John refers to was a nineteenth-century iron mill located approximately forty miles from Bangor in the town of Brownville. In *IT*, the ironworks are a primary setting referred to as the Kitchener Ironworks.

During the first half of the nineteenth century, Bangor was the lumber capital of America. In *The Tommyknockers*, King provides more of Derry's backstory in the chapter "The Town." Derry, mirroring Bangor's history, is where loggers did their drinking and whoring.

There were so many saloons, brothels and gambling houses located in one area of Bangor that it earned the moniker "Devil's Half Acre." John tells me the Bangor area has had a lot of death, and that it is imbedded in the soil. "When land and space on that land become tainted with death and destruction and negative mischief so to speak it's going to create that turmoil," he explains.

When I ask John if he had ever sensed anything supernatural or evil in Bangor, he tells me about the times he paddled the Penobscot River from Mount Katahdin to North Haven Island.

> *I think the most haunted part of the river, in my gut, is from Orono down to probably Hampden. I don't want to put my hand in the water, and I don't want to step on the shoreline from the canoe. I want to get through it. It has a feeling like you're in a really bad place. I'm afraid to look down. I don't dare to look in the water because I'm always thinking there will be a face there. That's the kind of feeling I get.*

Support Your Local Library

Year after year, Stephen and Tabitha King have shown their appreciation for libraries by awarding grants to libraries around the state of Maine through their foundation. In 1995, the Kings gave the Bangor Public Library $2.5 million to help renovate and expand the library's eighty-two-year-old brick and stone neoclassical building. They then challenged the city council and residents to help—and they did. In 2013, the Kings donated $3 million toward renovations, including repairs to the copper roof.

Stephen King has also gifted his fellow library-loving readers Mike Hanlon, a major protagonist in his book *IT*. As a child, Mike is a member of the Losers Club, a band of misfit kids in Derry who come together to fight Pennywise. He remains in Derry and becomes the town's librarian. Actors Marlon Taylor (young Mike) and Tim Reid (adult Mike) do him justice in the 1990 two-part miniseries adapted from the book.

As the resident local history expert, Mike's character educates members of the Losers Club and readers of *IT* about Derry. He recalls learning about a fire at the Black Spot, a Black officer's club in Derry that caught fire and burned everyone inside. There was an officer's club in Bangor, but it was not segregated, and no one died in a fire.

Mike recounts a local druggist telling him about the Bradley Gang shootout in Derry in 1929. The shootout is a fictionalized retelling of the real-life Brady Gang shootout that happened in Bangor in October 1937. Indiana

Bangor Public Library's current building opened to the public in 1913 and underwent major renovation in 1998. The King family has been instrumental in its success. *Photo by author.*

bank robber Al Brady was gunned down on Central Street in downtown Bangor by police officers and Federal Bureau of Investigation agents.

Mike describes a mass murder that took place in Derry in 1905. One of the victims was William Mueller, the owner of the Great Southern & Western Maine (GS&WM) train line. I don't know about a real-life mass murder in Bangor, but the GS&WM shows up in several of King's works, including "Rita Hayworth and the Shawshank Redemption" in the collection *Different Seasons* and the novella *Cycle of the Werewolf*. In *IT*, we learn from Losers Club member Eddie Kaspbrak's mother that the passenger trains ran from Boston, Massachusetts, through Portland and Derry all the way to Canada. Maine Central Railroad used to have a yard and roundhouse—where maintenance took place—in Bangor. It was the passenger and freight train service in Maine until the 1950s, when it began decreasing services.

SK TOURS

Welcome to Bangor, Welcome to Derry

As one of the tens of thousands of people who have taken the official Stephen King's Derry, Maine Tour, I can tell you with all honesty that it's a darn good time. So good I've taken it twice and plan to do it again. Jamie Tinker bought the business from his parents, Stu and Penney Tinker, and runs it with his wife, Jennifer. Their passion for all things King-related, knowledge of Bangor and King and sheer joy at having super fun jobs shines though. Each year, the tours change slightly because of new information Jamie and Jennifer were able to confirm. Some of the information gleaned on the tour comes directly from the source—Stephen and/or Tabitha King—by way of Stu Tinker.

Stories at least partially set in Derry:
IT
Insomnia
Bag of Bones
Dreamcatcher
"Fair Extension" from his collection *Full Dark, No Stars*
11/22/63

Stu Tinker owned and operated the legendary Betts Bookstore for twenty years. The shop specialized in King books and memorabilia. The location for the first eleven years was 25 Main Street, where Paddy Murphy's pub currently resides.

On April 17, 1974, Stu and Penney went to King's second signing ever. It was for *Carrie*, and by the grace of everything, Jamie's mother convinced his dad to spend $5.95 on a hardcover of the book and get it signed. Since then, there has been a kinship between Stu and King.

In 1984, the Tinkers started a limousine business. From there, a King's Bangor tour business started up. At first, family vehicles were used, but then they gravitated to commercial vans, which accommodate twice as many passengers.

Welcome Aboard

Jamie Tinker stands in the driveway of a two-story white house that would be unassuming if not for the maroon van with a monster clown on the side parked in the driveway. That vehicle is named Stu Redman, after a protagonist from *The Stand*. Parked behind it are several other vehicles, including a black Lincoln Navigator named Randall Flagg after the antagonist in *The Stand* and the Dark Tower series and a Dodge Sprinter named Traveling Jack inspired by Jack Sawyer, the main protagonist of *The Talisman* (a novel King co-wrote with author Peter Straub).

During the next three hours, I see the pawnshop King frequented in his pre-*Carrie* days to feed his kids; a Victorian-era psychiatric hospital complex, which even from our brief drive through I can see is *stunning*; Mount Hope Cemetery, where King used to walk around and get names off of headstones for characters (phonebooks have been another past resource); and the Bangor Opera House, where the film adaptation of his novel *Firestarter* had its world premiere in 1984. The canals. The house

Sinister sewer grate at corner of Jackson and Union Streets as seen with SK Tours. The tour visits locations that inspired King's work and film locations. *Photo by author.*

that inspired Losers Club member Beverly Marsh's childhood home. Bass Park, which is Bassey Park in Derry. The 110-foot-high white Thomas Hill Standpipe and adjacent park where as a child Jamie would see King sitting on a bench writing on a yellow legal pad.

One of the two most popular places on the tour for people to get out and take photos is at the corner of Jackson and Union Streets. This is the location of a special sewer grate. A grate so special Jamie has set a Pennywise mask and severed arm prop down on top of it. This is where in the first pages of *IT* an innocent little boy in a yellow rain jacket sails his wax-covered paper boat in the rain-filled street gutters. He meets Pennywise, and thus one of the most iconic scenes in horror storytelling history commences.

After taking many photos, we proceed to the King family's former home— the red brick house. We take more photos and then, with the promise of unlimited time in the gift shop, head back to SK Tours headquarters.

The tour does not go inside any buildings. There is a lot of ground to cover, and they do it well, but you do need to keep moving. At a few sites, you are able to get out and take photographs.

Keep in mind, these tours book up fast! Make sure to reserve as far in advance as possible. If you're unsure whether to sign up for a private tour or a public one, just ask Jamie and Jennifer. Save time for the home base's gift shop at 872 Hammond Street. Oh, and if you go, make sure to have Jamie tell you about the park benches down at the corner across from the airport.

BOB DUCHESNE—BIRD LOVER

First and foremost, Bob Duchesne is a birder, and because King makes a lot of bird references in his books, I thought it only prudent to talk to him.

For a long, long time Bob Duchesne was a radio host. Thirty-one years in fact. He was so good at it, the Country Music Association tapped him as America's Broadcast Personality of the Year in 1994. A decade later, shortly after retiring, he was inducted into the Country DJ Hall of Fame. From the broadcast booth, he ventured to the State House in Maine, where he served a dozen years in the Maine House of Representatives. During part of the time Bob was there, he sat on the Environment & Natural Resources and Inland Fisheries & Wildlife Committees.

Around 2000, he developed the Maine Birding Trail and site mainebirdingtrail.com. The site is chock-full of local knowledge, helping birders figure out when to go where based on tides and pests and where to find certain types of birds. These days he serves as vice president of Maine Audubon's Penobscot Valley Chapter and writes a weekly birding column for the *Bangor Daily News*.

Bob was born and raised in New Hampshire, came to Maine for college in 1971 and stayed. He became a birder in first grade.

I remember to this day looking out the window at all these goldfinches that came out onto the lawn after the rain. They were all over the lawn and so bright yellow. I was barely able to look out the window on my tiptoes, but I was absolutely fascinated by them.

He says it was a big enough event that his ninety-three-year-old mother remembers it to this day.

In fourth grade, he went up Mount Cardigan in the White Mountains of New Hampshire and heard a lot of white-throated sparrows. "That eerie whistling sound really haunted me, and it turns out my wife, who is a couple years younger, had the same experience on the same mountain," he shares.

High school brought sightings of cedar waxwings eating the berries off the mountain ash tree just outside the window of the library. The bird, an especially attractive one, is so named, Bob tells me, because of the bright red dots of wax-like material found on some of their feathers.

It all really started, though, with artist and ornithologist Roger Tory Peterson's pocket-size *Field Guide to the Birds*. Bob got a used copy and would check off the birds he saw. He has remained fascinated by birds for his entire life. "I just like going for walks, and I don't even have to see the bird. I know them when I hear them so it's just nice to have my friends around," he tells me.

The traditional way to identify a bird, Bob says, is the color and field marks. Once you get more skilled at it, you also start to identify habitat and behavior. You learn the songs. "I finally got good at birding by ear, just because I was annoyed that I could not identify them," he shares. "These days I know just about every noise a bird can make in Maine."

And there are some really cool ones. The American bittern—they're like an old-fashioned cast-iron well pump. They call it the thunder-pumper. Barred owls, of course, hoot, "Who cooks for you?" starting in late February or March. They mate early, and they start talking to each other and they also tell other owls to stay out of their territory. I highly recommend you check out the Cornell Lab Bird Cams online recording of a couple barred owls hooting.

Crow Roosts

We have a phenomenon going on right now. Crows are starting to do a lot of communal roosting right in towns, and there are probably, oh, five thousand crows that descend on the neighborhood next to the Kenduskeag Stream in downtown Bangor every night to roost. It's just astounding to watch that many birds, especially crows, sitting up there in the trees as the sun sets.

They are down by the Bangor Public Library and along the Kenduskeag Stream. They start to gather in October and November and for the most part disperse by April.

Bob tells me they've deemed it as safer in the city for them, because humans don't really hunt them or shoot them the way that they used to. It's a little bit warmer and brighter in town. They hate predators like owls, because great horned owls will snack on a crow every chance they get. Together they can watch for trouble, and he says they seem to exchange a little information about where the best food sources are. They eat just about everything, and that's another reason they like being around people in the winter. There is a lot of discarded food around human habitation. A tipped-over garbage can is a banquet. He says, "They're so smart."

Bats Are Adorable

"Bats are pretty cute," Bob shares. "The old wives' tales about them are way overblown. We have eight varieties in Maine. Some migrate, some overwinter in the eaves of your attic or tree hollows. A lot more around than you might think. They've suffered in recent years due to white-nose syndrome—a fungal growth affecting hibernating bats. They've really declined, but they are still out there."

Bob says the University of Maine has equipment so humans can hear bat sounds in our audible range. He has accessed the equipment twice and is astounded by what can be picked up.

Northern Maine Birds

"Maine is in a transition zone," he explains. "The forty-fifth parallel, midway between the North Pole and the Equator, runs right over the top of Old Town. Everything north of that shows what the Canadian forest is going to be like. You see more balsams and spruces and cedars. It gets more coniferous as you head north, and there is a whole set of birds north of Bangor that are not south of Bangor. I just love chasing those birds."

Spruce grouse is his favorite northern Maine bird. Bob says they are clowns and very tame, tending to be in the same place every time he visits. North of Bangor are different woodpeckers than in southern Maine. Canada jays, otherwise known as gray jays, are also only found in northern Maine.

We have two species of Chickadees in the state. The black-capped is the official state bird, but there is also the brown-capped one called the boreal chickadee that's north of Bangor. So, all that is going on in the northern half of the state, and I love getting out on those really remote logging roads where nobody else goes or even dares go and wandering around. I go in the deep woods and do it a lot.

Coastal Maine

Millions of years ago when the continents collided, Maine was a collision point. When that broke apart, it left the rock-bound coast a jagged mess that was ground down later by glaciers.

We have an incredibly rugged coastline with all those islands and that creates a lot of sheltered bays and coves that waterfowl and other seabirds get into. We have our iconic Atlantic puffin. There are five nesting islands off the coast of Maine and that's as far south as they get. Our ocean is weird. Our coastline is weird. The Gulf of Maine is abnormally cold because glaciers dumped a lot of silt out there—maybe one hundred miles offshore—so it's really shallow and tracks cold air. All that created the cold Gulf of Maine. You have that change of the Appalachian southern hardwood forest up into the coniferous Canadian forest right around the forty-fifth parallel. It is the most forested state in the nation. Lot of it taken away from the Natives and then privatized right away before Maine was even a state.

Some of the Birds in the Stephen King Universe

The Stand: crow
"Rita Hayworth and the Shawshank Redemption": pigeon
IT: A protagonist by the name of Stanley Uris is an avid bird watcher. Sparrows, blue jay, pair of robins, scarlet tanager, cardinal, grackle, bluebird, cowbird, golden eagle, auk
The Dark Half: sparrows
Needful Things: a parakeet

Want to do a bit of birding in northern Maine? Check out the Fields Pond Audubon Center located seven miles southeast of Bangor, in Holden and Orrington. The sanctuary encompasses 190 acres of fields, wetlands, forest and lakeshore frontage. There are several trail options, including the Lake Shore Trail and Fields Pond Audubon Center Loop. Details can be found at https://maineaudubon.org/visit/fields-pond/ and www.alltrails.com/trail/us/maine/fields-pond-audubon-center-loop.

ROBERT TALBOT—SPIRITUALIST

I pass underneath the metal arches with CAMP ETNA written on them and feel as if I am traveling from the present into the past.

My trip to the tiny town of Etna (population 1,208 in 2018) is because while King based his fictional town of Derry on Bangor, he distinguishes between the two towns in his stories. He locates Derry and Bangor close to each other. I believe Etna, which sits about twenty miles west of Bangor, may have inspired the setting of Derry.

Etna is associated with Camp Etna, a seasonal spiritualist community. A bucolic retreat founded over a century ago, it sits so far out of the way some locals don't know it exists. For someone like King though, who immerses himself in the history of places, I don't see how he could have missed it.

Robert Talbot, a sixth-generation spiritualist, invites me to meet with him on the screened porch of his purple cottage on the wooded campground. Sitting in a one-hundred-year-old rocking chair, watching hummingbirds flitter by, Robert presents a history of the camp and the movement whose

Camp Etna, a spiritualist camp in Etna, Maine. *Photo by author.*

followers believe that spirits of deceased people continue to live on after physical death.

At some point in their lives, Queen Victoria, writer Sir Arthur Conan Doyle, artist Hilma af Klint and inventor Thomas Edison all were attracted to spiritualism.

Welcome to Camp Etna!

As spiritualist camps go, Camp Etna is one of the three big ones left from the movement's Victorian-era heyday. Lily Dale, in New York, and Cassadaga, in Florida, are the others. All were founded in the mid- to late 1870s in the interest of bringing people working as mediums and psychics together. Thousands of people still visit these camps annually. Camp Etna is the smallest, having peaked during the early 1900s. A fire in 1922 destroyed 83 of the 130 cottages. Today, 50 cottages, not all of which are habitable, make up the campground.

The camp played a pivotal role in the study and promotion of physical phenomenon and spirit communication in the early years of spiritualism. In addition, the camp was involved with women's rights, and camp members were active in the political issues of the day. Over its long history, the camp has continued its strong support of students engaged in developing their mediumship and healing abilities.

The practice of spiritualism has evolved over time to still be here. So much of it is on thin ice in some ways. We're not. We're still here somehow, which is great.

Robert says people come to the camp during the summer season because they read about it in an article or book. They come to talk to a medium and connect with those who have passed, for psychic readings, for spiritual wellness and to enjoy the healing powers of nature. The camp offers table tipping, which is something I would love to try. Table tipping involves a group of people sitting around a small table. The participants place their hands palm down on the table and wait to see if it will be moved by a spirit.

Inherited Spirit

Robert grew up in the town of Stoneham, Massachusetts. His mother was a non-practicing spiritualist. His dad was a spiritualist at heart who was into theosophy, a popular late nineteenth-century religious movement, and reincarnation. He also studied astrology for over fifty years.

Generations of Robert's family were involved with the National Spiritual Alliance, a national spiritualist organization founded in 1913 in Lake Pleasant, Massachusetts. Members believe in mediumship and reincarnation. His great-great-grandmother was a founding member of the Alliance and a medium. His great-grandmother and grandmother were also mediums.

As a child, Robert had many events where he sensed something before it happened.

Mediums vs. Psychics

"A lot of people can be psychic, but not everybody can be a medium," Robert says. "But all mediums are psychics." Mediums use their intuitive abilities to read the energy around a sitter—or receive information from spirit(s) they pass on to the sitter. Mediums can communicate with people on the other side.

"Believe me, when you're on, it is beautiful," he explains. "I am the most skeptical medium you'll ever meet. It's hard for people to read me, number one. And number two, I always want verification."

"We can only give them what comes to us; [the] spirit is never wrong," he adds regarding mediumship.

A psychic is also intuitive but relies more on information they receive from non-physical vibrations.

Passing Under the Arches

It's like sliding into home plate in baseball terms and you feel safe. Oh, I made it. I feel comfortable here, and that's what people are attracted to. There is a lot of healing.

Robert says he feels energy when he walks around the campground. He used to walk barefoot around the land and the feeling was even more pronounced. He also feels a familiarity that comes from the people who are and have been there. The first person he met was from his hometown in Massachusetts. The cottage he lives in was once owned by a teacher he had in high school. "Is this coincidence, or are we all kind of related in the energy we want?" Robert declares.

He talks about how some people are drawn to the place to talk to the dead or for healing, but some arrive and don't know. "People have an opportunity to walk through the gates, even if they don't know why, they feel that peace when they come here," Robert says. "And they are astounded by that feeling. You watch the faces change."

Robert describes spiritualism as being like anything. "It is many colors," he tells me. "Everybody would have a different view. At the core spiritualists have a belief in the afterlife and the ability to communicate with it. There is continuity of life from here to the other side."

For a deep dive into the spiritualist movement and Camp Etna, there is no better source than writer Mira Ptacin's exquisite book *The In-Betweens: The Spiritualists, Mediums, and Legends of Camp Etna.*

11
HAVEN

SEASIDE TOWN: BUCKSPORT

L ike many Mount Desert Island–bound folks traveling the rugged coast of Maine, I gave the town of Bucksport no more than a passing glance as I continued right on Route 1 after crossing over the Penobscot River on my way to Bar Harbor. I made that trip several times before someone told me I should stop in Bucksport and check out the Dairy Port, an ice cream shop that has been around since the 1950s. And the next trip that's just what I did, needing no better reason than a cone of soft-serve ice cream.

Bucksport has a charming, if tiny, downtown waterfront area. Also, the town has a reputation for being one of the most haunted in Maine. This is largely due to stories about the cursed tomb of town founder Colonel Jonathan Buck. Sometime after a graveyard monument was erected in his honor in the mid-nineteenth century—decades after his death—a mysterious stain that looks like a boot appeared on the stone. One of the more popular variations goes that the colonel sentenced a woman to death for practicing witchcraft, and right before she was killed, she cursed him.

In King's novel *Pet Sematary*, set in the fictional town of Ludlow (based on the real town of Orrington), supporting characters Jud and Norma Crandall head to Bucksport to look at a dresser at the Emporium Galorium (a shop located in fictional Castle Rock in "The Sun Dog") and lunch at McLeod's. In real life, that would be MacLeod's Restaurant, a fine-dining establishment in Bucksport owned by George MacLeod, who went to school at the University of Maine in Orono with King.

Horror fans may know Bucksport as the real-life inspiration for Collinsport—the fictional setting of the popular 1960s gothic television series *Dark Shadows* created by horror visionary Dan Curtis.

Whether Bucksport also inspired King's fictional town of Haven, the setting of his novel *The Tommyknockers*, I am less sure—thinking the rural town of Montville is also a good fit. King includes a "1963 Total Eclipse of the Sun—Maine map" in both his novels *Gerald's Game* and *Dolores Claiborne*, placing Haven where Bucksport is.

However, in *The Tommyknockers*, the small town of Haven is described as being in a wooded area with old logging roads around and bordering the real town of Albion. King's history of the town has it beginning as the Montville Plantation in 1816.

Montville borders Albion and has a few logging roads around. It was incorporated in 1807 from the Davistown Plantation, which the Montville Historical Society says is referred to as the Montville Plantation. By the 1940s, the local mill had burned down, and there was not much left of the other small industries. Between 1950 and 1961, the Haystack Mountain School of Crafts was opened and ran there before relocating to the coast of Deer Isle. It has since become one of the premier art schools in the country.

Mixed-media artist and sculptor Barbara Fletcher, who studied at Haystack, completed a series of fantasy fabric sculptures for the Kings' former home in Bangor. The pieces combine brightly painted insects, animals, fish, flora and fauna. A number were (and may still be) suspended over their indoor pool.

Fright at the Fort

Fort Knox is a Civil War–era fort located in the town of Prospect, across the Penobscot River from Bucksport. It was constructed between 1844 and 1869 in response to concerns of British attack after the War of 1812 and Aroostook War. Soldiers were trained but never garrisoned there.

Dean Martin has been executive director of the Friends of Fort Knox since 2018. He started a few weeks before the organization's biggest annual fundraising event—Fright at the Fort. And as a King fan, he was positively giddy, because the theme was Stephen King. That event drew thousands of people who navigated multiple "scare zones," including one where strobe machine and tentacle arms reached out of the darkness ("The Mist") and a reproduction of the hobbling scene from *Misery*.

An enthusiastic man by nature—as we walk around the fort venturing into the simmering sunshine then ducking back into dark passageways—he makes jokes and gushes excitedly about recent and upcoming events, including Civil War encampments and ghost camps. He talks about how the pentagonal fort is primarily made of granite from a local quarry, that "Two-Step Alley" is a walkway leading along the inside of the fort's walls, the master craftsmanship involved in creating multistory spiral staircases and Sergeant Leopold Hegyi, a Hungarian immigrant who became the caretaker of the fort between 1887 and 1900. His ghost reportedly still walks his rounds again and again—though his grave is in nearby Stockton Springs.

Upstairs at the Alamo

The Alamo Theatre, a first-run 140-seat movie theater, has been a Main Street Bucksport fixture off and on for the last century. The second floor of the Alamo Theatre building is Northeast Historic Film's home.

Oregon-born executive director and co-founder David S. Weiss came to Maine by way of Boston, where he worked in the production house trenches of commercial audio-visual work. During what he describes as an experimental year in 1984 with his ex-wife Karan Sheldon in Blue Hill, they looked for production work in Maine. What they found, by way of the University of Maine, was *Stump to Ship*, an amateur silent film of Maine's woodsmen from 1930. They took on the preservation of the film with a small team and then exhibited to sold-out shows around the state.

Karan and David realized everybody has film and nobody knows what it is or what to do with it. They decided to become film archivists, consulted with the film archivist at the Museum of Modern Art in New York, put out a press release and began working out of a cramped makeshift office at home.

It was let's do another one like it. Hey, I wonder whose got all the old film. And that was the fatal question. Every institution "We have a few boxes of things, but we don't really know what's in them. We don't have the people, time, etc." And then people would come up from the audience and say, "I've got film like that." The phone started ringing. I'm moving to Florida if you can get here by Friday, you can have the stuff, I've been collecting for thirty years.

In 1992, they moved the archive to a large boarded-up building in Bucksport. A three-story climate-controlled vault was added along the way—holding at least twelve million feet of film, including famed author E.B. White's home movies. The writer of *Charlotte's Web* and *Stuart Little* loved animals and photographed from the ground up. Academy Award–nominated documentary filmmaker Ken Burns has sourced material from Northeast Historic Film.

A Local's Tale

To Alamo Theatre manager Jane Donnell, Stephen King is a real person—"He's the guy who built the baseball field in Bangor," she says.

"I'm a Maine girl, and Stephen King has been woven into my life from reading short stories with my best friend as little kids," Jane shares. One of the early King stories she recalls unnerving her is the short story "I Am the Doorway" from his collection *Night Shift*, which involves hands with eyeballs.

Her college roommate's brother was a stand-in for one of King's movies. Her aunt babysat for the Kings when they rented a house in Orrington, while King was teaching at UMaine in Orono.

During the summer of 1990, she occasionally gave the younger brother of one of her favorite high school teachers a ride to his summer job in the old Army National Guard Armory in Brewer. That's where the rats were housed for the film adaptation of King's short story "Graveyard Shift." "All he did all day was sit in this tent with the rats to make sure they were OK and had water and stuff," she says.

When the theater needed to go digital in 2014 because it was getting harder to get 35mm prints, she approached the town for help funding the new projector system.

The Kings, having read about this little town trying to save their one-screen movie theater, stepped forward. The Kings said you have so much skin in the game that we will match any more donations. That was amazing. King isn't in a lot of people's lives directly except when he's helping you keep your job and keep your town.

Appendix

MY TOWN

THREE-DAY ITINERARIES

Getting here: Concord Coach Lines, Greyhound, Amtrak's Downeaster, Portland Jetport (PWM) and Bangor International Airport (BGR). Note, you will need a car to venture outside of Portland.

Following are a couple of three-day itineraries that focus on the geographic areas covered in this book.

All information is current as of January 21, 2024. It's recommended that you check online for the most up-to-date pricing and hours.

ITINERARY NO. 1 (PORTLAND, DURHAM, LISBON FALLS, LEWISTON, BRIDGTON)

DAY ONE PORTLAND, CASCO BAY

Kick off your trip with a coffee and a hearty breakfast sandwich at TANDEM COFFEE AND BAKERY (742 Congress Street | www.tandemcoffee.com). For more typical diner food, look no further than BECKY'S (390 Commercial Street | http://beckysdiner.com/BeckysMenu.pdf). Since 1991, it's been a place of reverence for local fishermen because of the hearty portions of pancakes and eggs and low prices. Prefer a menu with lots of organic, vegan and gluten-free options? LB KITCHEN (255 Congress Street | www. lbkitchenportlandme.com) has you covered. Treat yourself to a house chai and the avocado toast.

One of the best ways to introduce yourself to Maine is to take advantage of the CASCO BAY LINES MAILBOAT TOUR (56 Commercial Street | www. cascobaylines.com). This true working boat carries passengers, mail and freight to Little Diamond, Great Diamond, Long, Cliff and Chebeague Islands. A local favorite, the trip takes a little over three hours. It runs daily year-round. There are no concessions on board, so consider packing snacks and drinks, sunscreen and a windbreaker.

While Stephen King is unlikely to have found inspiration from any of these islands for his fictional Tall Island, I can guarantee you that Dolores Claiborne (protagonist of his novel *Dolores Claiborne*) would feel quite at home.

What's Near the Ferry Terminal

STANDARD BAKING CO. (75 Commercial Street | https://standardbakingco. com). This popular bakeshop offers European-style breads and pastries, including the not-to-miss prosciutto and asiago croissant.

SEA BAGS flagship store (123 Commercial Street | https://seabags.com). These totes made from recycled sails are as sturdy as they are stylish.

FISH & BONE (5 India Street | https://www.thefishandbone.com). This pet shop specializes in treats for your very own Cujo, or Church, the cat.

MAINE NARROW GAUGE RAILROAD (49 Thames Street | https:// mainenarrowgauge.org). From May to October, this family-friendly train welcomes visitors aboard daily for a forty-minute ride, which includes views of Casco Bay.

EASTERN PROMENADE TRAIL (https://trails.org/our-trails/eastern-prom-trail). Built along an old rail corridor, this paved waterfront trail starts where Commercial Street ends. Benches and picnic tables are located along the route and at East End Beach, which is a great place to kick back with a good Stephen King book. Several food trucks operate in Fort Allen Park, which runs above the trail.

After your cruise head to NOVARE RES BIER CAFÉ (188 Middle Street | https://novareresbiercafe.com), a must-stop for beer aficionados. The bar is located in the Old Port District, the historic section of downtown where cobblestone streets weave among red brick buildings. Nearby you'll find the HUNT AND ALPINE (75 Market Street | https://www.huntandalpineclub. com), Portland's premier cocktail destination and a great spot for small bites. My favorite combo is the citrusy Green Eyes gin-based cocktail and spicy popcorn.

Happy Meals

For dinner, I often take friends to EVENTIDE OYSTER CO. (86 Middle Street | www.eventideoysterco.com), which is always packed and doesn't take reservations. Locals and visitors alike go for their fresh-from-the-docks oysters. I'm a huge fan of the fried oyster bun and pickled vegetable salad with nori vinaigrette.

In the West End neighborhood, my go-to place is the Japanese restaurant PAI MEN MIYAKE (188 State Street | https://www.miyakerestaurants.com/ menus/paimen). I cannot get enough of the Brussels sprouts and ramen. A fan of super creative cocktails in a delightful space featuring murals and a bookcase with plants? Then afterward head over to the JEWEL BOX (644 Congress Street | https://www.jewelboxportlandmaine.com) for a creative nightcap like Space Moth (smoky scotch, crème de violette, orange bitters and ginger/honey syrup).

When figuring where to eat, locals will guide you to the website Portland Food Map. It's the go-to resource for dining in this foodie town: https:// www.portlandfoodmap.com.

Seafood with a View

Feel like a drive? THE LOBSTER SHACK at Two Lights in Cape Elizabeth (225 Two Lights Road | https://lobstershacktwolights.com) has been a local landmark since the 1920s. Open April–October with the promise of items like steamed Maine lobsters and haddock sandwiches. The picnic tables with a view of the coast are pretty darn spectacular.

If you have time—PORTLAND MUSEUM OF ART (7 Congress Square | www.portlandmuseum.org/homer). The collection of over eight thousand artworks includes pieces by three generations of Wyeths, Alex Katz and Lois Dodd. The museum also offers tours of Winslow Homer's Studio in nearby

Prouts Neck from early May to mid-November. Reservations for the two-and-a-half-hour tours, which include transportation to the studio, should be booked well in advance.

Book It

Green Hand Bookshop (661 Congress Street | https://greenhandbookshop. com). New and used stock including plenty of vintage King, large weird fiction and horror sections. Bonus: Joe's Super Variety, the family-owned convenience store across the street, makes appearances in a few of King's books.
Coast City Comics (634 Congress Street | https://coastcitycomics.com). King character figurines and floor-to-ceiling cases of comics.
Longfellow Books (1 Monument Square | www.longfellowbooks.com). Check out the staff recommendations or consult Meg, the store manager, who has turned me on to a few fantasy reads.
Sherman's Maine Coast Book Shop (49 Exchange Street | www.shermans. com). In addition to new releases and popular fiction, you can find a large selection of books about Maine.
Casablanca Comics (151 Middle Street, lower level | https:// casablancacomics.com). The shop carries a solid selection of graphic novels and vintage sets of comics.
Print: A Bookstore (273 Congress Street | www.printbookstore.com). Pulitzer Prize–winning author Richard Russo founded this delightful shop, where there is usually an ample selection of King's books and a stellar stock of titles by local authors. Be sure to check out their Events page.
Maine Historical Society shop (489 Congress Street | www.mainehistory. org/plan-your-visit/mhs-store/). Fabulous stock of Maine literature, historical books, cookbooks and more. Tour the Wadsworth-Longfellow House next door.

Day Two Durham, Lisbon Falls, Lewiston

Before hitting the road, fill up on buttermilk waffles with real Maine maple syrup at Hot Suppa (703 Congress Street | http://hotsuppa.com). Afterward, head a few blocks over to Portland's West End neighborhood, where you can check out stately Victorian-era homes. On the Western Promenade, get a glimpse at Maine Medical Center, where King was born.

If you'd rather sleep in, swing by HiFi Donuts (30 City Center | https://hifidonuts.com) and then hit the road. Grab some strong coffee and a honey-glazed cake donut.

Depending on traffic, the drive from Portland to Durham is around thirty-five minutes via 295 N and ME-125 N. Follow the self-guided driving tour outlined in the Durham chapter or punch Durham Get & Go or 697 Royalsborough Road into your GPS. The tour can take anywhere from thirty minutes to an hour depending on how many times you stop for photos.

Have a Castle Rock Moment

Take in the town where Stephen King spent time as a youth.

In Lisbon Falls, stop by Little River Coffee (11 Union Street | https://lrcoffeeco.com) for a lavender latte and say hi to owners Maggie and Kate. Their brownies and gluten-free bars are incredible.

Little Androscoggin River outside Mechanic Falls, a small town about ten miles west of the L-A area. Is referenced in stories, including *Salem's Lot. Photo by author.*

Afterward, don't miss the MAINE ART GLASS STUDIO AND SANCTUARY GALLERY (51 Main Street | www.facebook.com/MaineArtGlassStudio) or the bug museum upstairs. Stained glass works and supplies for sale.

If you think you'll be in Lisbon Falls after 5:00 p.m., do yourself a favor and make a reservation at FLUX RESTAURANT AND BAR (12 Main Street | www.fluxnomnom.com). I'm devoted to their tempura cauliflower. Can't get a reservation? Then get your food to go. Just down the block is OLIVE PIT BREWING (16 Main Street | www.olivepitbrewing.com). The pub is named after the owners' beloved pit bull Olive Roo. Well behaved, leashed pets are welcome in the taproom and beer garden.

L-A time

Get back on the road and head over to artsy Lewiston. It is about a twenty-minute drive from Lisbon Falls. Your next stop is the PUBLIC THEATRE, where King used to watch monster movies as a kid. Check out https://thepublictheatre.org for dates of shows and events.

Just a few blocks away, is—King approved—SIMONES' HOT DOG STAND (99 Chestnut Street). Open weekdays 8:00 a.m. to 2:00 p.m. If you're visiting on a Saturday, you'll want to slide into a booth at ROLLY'S DINER (87 Mill Street | https://rollysnewauburn.com) and dine like a local. I go for the veggie omelet with home fries and toast.

Want to learn a bit about Lewiston's fascinating industrial history? Don't miss the MAINE MUSEUM OF INNOVATION, LEARNING AND LABOR (35 Canal Street | https://mainemill.org).

Need a pick-me-up? Check out BLUE JAY COFFEE (189 Main Street | www.bluejaycoffee.me). Owner Jenna Guiggey makes knockout lattes with her own in-house flavors. Hang out in the book- and plant-friendly sunlit spot or take your coffee to go book hunting.

QUIET CITY BOOKS (124 Lisbon Street | www.facebook.com/CourtneyQuietCity/) has a great selection of used books and an adoptable kitty via a partnership with the Greater Androscoggin Humane Society.

For dinner, you have options: FISH BONES GRILL (70 Lincoln Street | https://fishbonesgrill.com) in Lewiston or MAC'S DOWNEAST SEAFOOD (894 Minot Avenue | https://macsdowneastseafood.com) in neighboring Auburn.

If you have time—the BRUNSWICK NAVAL AVIATION MUSEUM (https://bnamuseum.org). King references the former station in several stories. In *Salem's Lot*, an air force kid is waiting for the bus at the local Greyhound station.

Recommended Stephen King reading before visiting Durham and Lisbon Falls: *Salem's Lot, The Dead Zone, Different Seasons (The Body), Needful Things, 11/22/63, Revival, Gwendy's Button Box* and *Elevation*.

DAY THREE BRIDGTON

Roll down your windows and set out on the thirty-nine-mile drive from Portland to Bridgton via US-302. This is the reverse route some of the main characters take at the end of King's 1980 novella *The Mist*. Be sure to pull over in Naples for a photo of Long Lake, which is also featured in the book.

As you pull into downtown, Renys Department Store (151 Main Street | www.renys.com) will be on your left. James Rennie Sr., one of the primary antagonists of King's novel *Under the Dome*, was named after the store. Be sure to pop in for anything and everything from saltwater taffy to lobster fridge magnets.

My Favorite Spots in Town

BETH'S KITCHEN CAFÉ (108 Main Street | https://bethskitchencafe.com). It's all good, especially the French onion soup and the cobb salad. Also, the Speckled Ax brand wood-roasted coffee is fine.

PLATT DESIGNS (32 Main Street | https://plattdesignsforthehome.com). The charming stock at this interior decorating shop is matched only by the family that owns it. Bonus, it is located in the William F. Perry House—a nineteenth-century example of transitional Italianate–Second Empire architecture.

BRIDGTON BOOKS (140 Main Street | https://www.bridgtonbooks.com) King makes a beeline here when in the area. Mostly new books. Solid Stephen King paperback selection—surprise, some may be signed! Bonus, the shop has a sweet kitty in residence.

Afterward, drive over to the PEABODY-FITCH FARM (46 Narramissic Road | www.lelt.org/peabody-fitch-woods). It was built in 1797 by one of the town's first settlers, and the Bridgton Historical Society runs tours June through August (www.bridgtonhistory.org). Loon Echo Land Trust maintains two and a half miles of scenic trails around the farm. During deer hunting season, which runs from late October through early

December, wear a bright orange article of clothing. If you'll be traveling with a dog, put a vest or bandana on them too.

Hanging out in Bridgton after dark? I recommend the old-school drive-in experience courtesy of BRIDGTON TWIN DRIVE-IN (383 Portland Road). The place is a cinematic institution in Maine's Lakes Region. In addition to new releases, they have retro nights.

If you have time—OXFORD BEER GARDEN (420 Main Street Oxford | https://oxbowbeer.com/location/oxford), where you can eat delicious wood-fired pizza and drink finely crafted beer in a two-hundred-year-old barn. Or hit up downtown Norway for a little shopping (my favorites are FIBER & VINE for wine, HANDMADE MAINE for gifts, the RAVEN COLLECTIONS for crystals and FOOD FOR THOUGHT for used books—I've scored a few of King's works here). Fill up on coffee culture at local favorite CAFÉ NOMAD (450 Main Street Norway | www.cafenomad.com).

Depending on when you go, spend a day at the FRYEBURG FAIR—Maine's Blue Ribbon Classic Agricultural Fair (www.fryeburgfair.org) held in early October. Just to be safe, assume everything but fair admission and rides will be cash only. This is King's favorite Maine fair. Fryeburg is about fifteen miles from Bridgton via Route 302.

Recommended King reading before visiting Bridgton: *The Mist* and *Under the Dome*.

ITINERARY NO. 2 (ORONO, BANGOR)

DAY ONE BANGOR

Once known as the "Lumber Capital of the World," Bangor has reinvented itself in the last century. It is the commercial center of northern Maine, a small walkable city with a bounty of downtown restaurants.

The first thing any Stephen King fan visiting Bangor is going to want to do is check out King-related haunts. Succumb to temptation with the SK Tours of Maine driving tour of Bangor (https://sk-tours.com) During a three-hour tour, visitors will be introduced to various locations where King has lived and worked, places that have inspired his stories and film locations. Snag a selfie in front of the iconic bat and spider decorated front gates of King's former home. Tours begin at 9:00 a.m. and 2:00 p.m.

Afterward stop in Wicked Brew Café (173 Park Street) for a refreshing glass of freshly squeezed lemonade and the tuna salad wrap (https://wickedbrewcafe.co). Chimera Coffee is also a fine choice for a caffeinated pick me up and a pastry (https://www.chimeracoffeeco.com).

Read All about It

Next up, stroll over to the Bangor Public Library (145 Harlow Street). It is beloved by the King family. The brick and stone neoclassical building opened in 1913. My favorite places in the library are the collections room, standing in the lobby under the old copper dome and the foreign language section on the third floor. The library has a prodigious collection of Stephen King books with a variety of cool foreign covers.

Another option to the library is walking around downtown and taking in the historic architecture and shops. The Briar Patch bookstore at 27 Central Street and Rock and Art Shop at 36 Central Street are personal favorites. (https://buildingsofnewengland.com/category/maine/bangor/).

Past Tense

Early evening, take a peek into the past with the Bangor Historical Society. I have heard the Mount Hope Cemetery tour is especially well done. Built in 1834, the three-hundred-acre cemetery is the nation's second-oldest garden cemetery. King has been known to take names from tombstones for characters. The cemetery was also used to film a scene with King for the 1989 adaptation of his novel *Pet Sematary* (www.bangorhistoricalsociety.org/tours/).

Dining Out

For a Losers Club–worthy dinner, head over to Oriental Jade (320 Bangor Mall Boulevard | https://www.orientaljade.com) for the Pu Pu Platter (egg roll, teriyaki beef and chicken, boneless spare ribs, chicken wings, chicken fingers and seafood rangoon). In King's novel *IT*, which takes place in Derry (based on Bangor), several old friends who refer to themselves as the "Losers Club" reunite at a local Chinese restaurant. Years ago, when King spent more time in Bangor, he was known to have dinner at Oriental Jade before going to the movies at the adjacent mall.

If you're looking for something more in the fine-dining arena, you'll find it at KANÙ in the small town of Old Town on the bank of the Penobscot River. Just a twenty-minute drive from Bangor, Old Town is where author Tabitha King was born and raised and where the Kings got married. Across the river is Indian Island Reservation. Check out www.penobscotnation.org for details.

At KANÙ (283 Main Street | www.283kanu.com), indulge in one of their seasonal milkshakes (alcoholic and nonalcoholic options) topped with flavored whip cream and decorated with candy and mini baked treats. My pick for the winning entrée is the veggie burger served with a side of house chips. Gluten-free bun available.

DAY TWO ACADIA NATIONAL PARK OR ORRINGTON, BUCKSPORT AND CASTINE

It is all about options on your second day. Depending on your mood and the weather, you could drive the approximate one and half hours to ACADIA NATIONAL PARK for a hike. The fifty-thousand-acre outdoor playground is home to 363 types of birds (www.nps.gov/acad/learn/nature/birds.htm), making it one of the best bird-watching areas in the country.

Another option is to head to the charming coastal village of Castine via Bucksport and Orrington. Located about a one-hour drive from Bangor, Castine is home to a number of family-owned shops, art galleries and restaurants. The little town is also home to the Maine Maritime Academy. The twenty-acre waterfront campus includes the country's only surviving historic wooden shipyard, a Victorian shipbuilder's home and indoor galleries.

Note, with a few exceptions, these are seasonal offerings—Acadia's paved roads are closed from early December through mid-April. Coastal towns like Castine cater to "vacationlanders" (or as King likes to call them in his stories, "summer people") and thus begin to empty out and close up by mid-October.

Option One: Acadia National Park and Bar Harbor

Check out the National Park Service's tip page for visiting the park (www.nps. gov/acad/learn/news/top-ten-tips-for-your-visit-to-acadia-national-park.

htm). It's recommended you purchase your park entrance pass in advance. Note, a separate vehicle reservation is required for Cadillac Mountain. Pets are welcome but must be leashed. The Hulls Cove Visitor Center off Route 3 near Bar Harbor is Acadia's main visitor contact station and transportation hub from May into October. It opens at 8:30 a.m.

One of my favorite ways to see the park is from the cliffs with ACADIA MOUNTAIN GUIDES (https://acadiamountainguides.com/climb-acadia/). They have been operating in the park since 1993 with veteran climbers who are also certified at or above the wilderness first responder level of medical care. My advice is to do the four-hour option. That should give you plenty of time for a thorough experience.

I have never kayaked around Acadia, so I recommend checking out this site about boating there: www.nps.gov/acad/planyourvisit/boating.htm. There are several outfitters in the area with ample positive reviews.

Before you start your adventure, check out CAFÉ THIS WAY (14V2 Mt. Desert Street | Bar Harbor www.cafethisway.com). This local favorite is open daily from 6:30 a.m. to 1:00 p.m. My usual is The Usual (two eggs, home fries, sourdough toast and veggie sausage) with a cup of coffee. Bonus: bibliophiles, part of the café is lined with bookcases.

For dinner, head over to MCKAY'S PUBLIC HOUSE (231 Main Street | www.mckayspublichouse.com). It's all good, but the appetizer menu is especially appealing with the house-made soft pretzels with beer cheese fondue, the MDI mussels and brussels sprouts. A rotating selection of excellent Maine beers pairs nicely with all of the above dishes.

Option Two: Orrington, Bucksport, Castine

Journey south from Bangor into the rural countryside on Route 15, also known as River Road, to the town of Orrington, King's real-life inspiration for his fictional town of Ludlow where his novels *Pet Sematary* and *The Dark Half* take place. Note, Route 15, a busy two-lane country highway, is Route 5 in his fictional universe. And if you see any Cianbro Corporation trucks, those would be Orinoco company vehicles in his stories.

In 1978, while King was a writer in residence and professor at his alma mater, University of Maine at Orono, he and his family lived at 664 River Road. While there, an unfortunate family event spurred him to begin writing the novel *Pet Sematary* about a family whose pet cat is killed on the busy road. The family buries the cat in the pet cemetery in the woods behind the house.

In real life, there was a little pet cemetery behind 664 River Road with a sign a child is presumed to have misspelled "pet sematary" on.

The cemetery is on private property, and from what I hear, there's nothing left if you can even find it through the brambles. Fans found out about it and picked through it years ago. Also, the two-lane road is dangerously busy with folks driving entirely too fast—so be careful if you stop to take photos.

About thirty minutes farther south in the town of Prospect is FORT KNOX, one of the best-preserved historic forts on New England's coast (www. fortknoxmaine.com). It's just across the Penobscot River from Bucksport off Route 1. I detail the nineteenth-century fort in the Bucksport chapter.

At the fort, you can purchase tickets for the elevator ride to the top of the Penobscot Narrows Bridge Observatory next door. The observatory, which opened in 2007, is forty-two stories, making it the highest bridge observatory in the world. The 360-degree view offers a panoramic look at the historic fort and Penobscot Bay (www.maine.gov/mdot/pnbo/).

Following your high-altitude adventure, fuel up at CROSBY'S DRIVE-IN (30 Duck Cove Road in Bucksport). The menu features lobster rolls, haddock sandwiches, baskets of fried clams, fried pickles (the best I've ever had), hamburgers and veggie burgers. You can sit in your car or at one of the picnic tables with umbrellas.

Then it is on to Castine. Things to do include a harbor tour with *Tugboat Lil' Toot* (http://castinecruises.com). A dip at rocky-sand Wadsworth Cove Beach. At the north side of the entrance to Castine Harbor is the decommissioned and privately owned DICE HEAD LIGHTHOUSE (https:// visitmaine.com/things-to-do/lighthouses-sightseeing/dice-head).

Are you a reader looking for a book? Look no further than the COMPASS ROSE BOOKSTORE AND CAFÉ (3 Main Street | https://www. compassrosebookscastine.com). They focus on new books, Maine authors and children's books about Maine.

Feeling peckish? In the BREEZE AND CASTINE VARIETY at the corner of Main and Water Streets, you'll find a rotating selection of baked goods (https://www.facebook.com/castinevariety/). At DENNETT'S WHARF (15 Sea Street | https://www.dennetts.co), oysters, lobster (with corn and fries), chowders and baskets of fried seafood are on the menu.

Castine is about a three-hour drive from Portland, so you could always spend the night in town and then drive south and take advantage of some of the experiences I outline in the first itinerary. Or you could head back to Bangor and check out King's collegiate stomping grounds the following day.

Day Three Orono

Get caffeinated at The Ampersand Store (22 Mill Street Orono). It offers a variety of coffee and tea drinks, and the big fluffy baked goods practically fly out of the shop.

No more than a half day is needed to explore Orono, home to the University of Maine. Self-guided walking tours are available of the picturesque campus (https://umaine.edu/sights/). I recommend the Circle the Mall and Historic District tours. Tree-lined paths, ample green spaces, and historic buildings abound. Be sure to take time to admire Fogler Library, if only from the outside. This was where Stephen King met his future wife, Tabitha, as an undergrad. If you visit while school is in session September–May, parking could be harder to find.

Options for food in tiny downtown Orono include Thai Orchid (pan-Asian noodle dishes) and Pat's Pizza (I love the Hawaiian, featuring pineapple and ham).

If you have a few more days of vacation time available, consider a canoe trip with Mahoosuc Guide Service on the Penobscot River. During the Way of the Wabanaki trip, I learned about birchbark canoes, made a basket and went on a medicinal plant walk. The stories around the campfire at night were memorable. The food—salmon and fiddleheads and blueberry pie—is some of the best I've ever had. And the guides, treasures each and every one (https://mahoosuc.com/guided-canoe-trips/).

SOURCES

Bangor Public Library. "Bangor in Focus." https://bangorinfo.com/Focus/focus_bpl.html.

Bauman, John F. "Strathglass Park." Society of Architectural Historians. https://sah-archipedia.org.

Bellamann, Henry. *King's Row*. Houston, TX: Kingdom House, 1942.

Bertrand, Steve. Interview with Stephen King. "Meet the Writers." Barnes & Noble. YouTube. 1993. www.youtube.com/watch?v=ic7JnF4vStA.

Bridgton, Maine 1768–1994: An Updated Bicentennial History. Bridgton, ME: Bridgton Historical Society, 1993.

Buffalo News. "Woman Who Was Put in Morgue by Mistake Dies One Week Later." November 9, 1994. https://buffalonews.com.

Burnham, Emily. "Bangor Council Vote Lets Stephen and Tabitha King Move Ahead with Archive and Writers Retreat." *Bangor Daily News*, October 18, 2019. www.bangordailynews.com.

Butler, Joyce. *Wildfire Loose: The Week Maine Burned*. Camden, ME: Down East Books, 1997.

Cayer, Aaron. "Mill Supply: Making Paper and Maintaining the Technological Sublime." American Roundtable. https://archleague.org.

Farrin, Bruce. "Chisholm's Influence Still Seen in Rumford." *Sun Journal*, January 31, 2016. www.sunjournal.com.

Finkel, Laura. "UMaine During the Vietnam War Era: Guide to the UMaine during the Vietnam War era/Laura Finkel Collection." University of

Maine, Raymond H. Fogler Library, 2018. Part of the Northeast Archives of Folklore and Oral History Repository.

Fryeburg Fair: First 150 Years 1851–2000. Fryeburg, ME: West Oxford Agricultural Society, 2000.

Gendrolis, Emily. "Notes from the Archives. Grants Department Store." Maine Historical Society. April 28, 2014. https://mainehistory.wordpress.com.

Gould, John. *The House that Jacob Built*. Camden, ME: DownEast Books, 1945.

Greene, Andy. "Stephen King: The Rolling Stone Interview." *Rolling Stone*, October 31, 2014. www.rollingstone.com.

History. "Roswell." November 9, 2009. www.history.com.

King, Stephen. *Bag of Bones*. New York City: Scribner, 1998.

———. *The Bazaar of Bad Dreams*. New York: Scribner, 2015.

———. *Carrie*. New York: Doubleday, 1974.

———. *The Colorado Kid*. London: Titan Books, 2005.

———. *Cujo*. New York: Viking Press, 1981.

———. *Cycle of the Werewolf*. New York: Signet, 1985.

———. *Danse Macabre*. New York: Gallery Books, 2010.

———. *The Dark Half*. New York: Viking Press, 1989.

———. *The Dead Zone*. New York: Viking Press, 1979.

———. *Different Seasons*. New York: Viking Press, 1982.

———. *Dolores Claiborne*. New York: Viking Press, 1993.

———. *Dreamcatcher*. New York: Scribner, 2001.

———. *Elevation*. New York: Scribner, 2018.

———. *11/22/63*. New York: Scribner, 2011.

———. *Everything's Eventual*. New York: Scribner, 2002.

———. *Four Past Midnight*. New York: Viking Press, 1990.

———. *Gerald's Game*. New York: Viking Press, 1992.

———. *The Girl Who Loved Tom Gordon*. New York: Scribner, 1999.

———. *Gwendy's Button Box*. New York: Simon & Schuster, 2017.

———. *Hearts in Atlantis*. New York: Scribner, 1999.

———. *Holly*. New York: Scribner, 2023.

———. *Huffy*. "a not sermon." August 26, 1984.

———. *If It Bleeds*. New York: Scribner, 2020.

———. *Insomnia*. New York: Viking Press, 1994.

———. *The Institute*. New York: Scribner, 2019.

———. *IT*. New York: Viking Press, 1986.

———. *Just After Sunset*. New York: Scribner, 2008.

———. *Lisey's Story*. New York: Scribner, 2006.

———. *Needful Things*. New York: Viking Press, 1991.

———. *Nightmares & Dreamscapes*. New York: Viking Press, 1993.

———. *Night Shift*. New York: Doubleday, 1978.

———. "A Novelist's Perspective on Bangor." *Bangor Daily News*. April 11, 2018. http://bangordailynews.com.

———. *On Writing: A Memoir of the Craft*. New York: Scribner, 2010.

———. *Pet Sematary*. New York: Doubleday, 1983.

———. *Revival*. New York: Scribner, 2014.

———. *Salem's Lot*. New York: Doubleday, 1975.

———. *Skeleton Crew*. New York: Simon & Schuster, 1985.

———. *The Stand*. New York: Doubleday, 1978.

———. *The Tommyknockers*. New York: Simon & Schuster, 1987.

———. *Under the Dome*. New York: Scribner, 2009.

King, Stephen, and Richard Chizmar. *Gwendy's Final Task*. New York City: Simon & Schuster, 2022.

King, Stephen, Michael Alpert, Jim Bishop, David Bright and Keith Carreiro. *Hearts in Suspension*. Orono: University of Maine Press, 2016.

King, Tabitha. Updated by Marsha DeFilippo. "The Author." Stephen King official website. https://stephenking.com.

Kitchens, Sharon. "Stephen King's Maine." ArcGIS Online. Esri. Oct 2020. https://storymaps.arcgis.com.

LaFlamme, Mark. "Stephen King's Maine: 17 Curious Things about Lewiston, Durham, and Other King Haunts." *Lewiston Sun Journal*, July 29, 2018.

Leamon, James S. "Historic Lewiston: A Textile City in Transition." Lewiston Historical Commission, 1976. www.lewistonmaine.gov.

Lee, Russell. "1947: Year of the Flying Saucer." National Air and Space Museum, June 24, 2022. https://airandspace.si.edu.

Lewiston-Auburn District Telephone Directory. New England Telephone & Telegraph Company, 1954.

Lewiston, Town of. "History of Lewiston Maine." (2019). *Maine History Documents*. 213. https://digitalcommons.library.umaine.edu.

Lisbon Yearbook. 1965, 1967.

The Magic Lantern. www.magiclanternmovies.com.

Maine College of Art. "Porteous Building." www.meca.edu.

Maine Memory Network. William Arnold House in Bangor. www.mainememory.net.

Meander Maine. "The Public Theatre." https://meandermaine.com.

Metalious, Grace. *Peyton Place*. Boston: Northeastern University Press, 1956.

Meyer, Judith. "For Boy, Crime, Filth, Chaos and Love Were All Part of Life at 105-111 Blake." *Sun Journal*, August 11, 2013. www.sunjournal.com.

Morine, David. *Vacationland: A Half Century Summering in Maine*. Camden, ME: Down East Books, 2015.

Mount Hope Cemetery. https://mthopebgr.com.

Moxie Festival. www.moxiefestival.com.

National Park Service. Historic Preservation Survey Rumford, Maine. 1979. https://npgallery.nps.gov.

Nellie Ruth "Ruthie Pill" Pillsbury King. Find a Grave. www.findagrave.com.

Nelson, Shirley. *Fair, Clear and Terrible: The Story of Shiloh, Maine*. Eugene, OR: Wipf and Stock, 1989.

Norman, Melora. "Maine Library History." *Maine Policy Review* 22, no. 1 (2013): 20–30. https://digitalcommons.library.umaine.edu.

Online Encyclopedia. "Maine Central Railroad Company." www.encyclopedia.com.

Platz & Associates. Bates Mill. www.platzassociates.com.

Plummer, Francis W. *Lisbon: The History of a Small Maine Town*. Lisbon Falls, ME: 1970.

Portland Women's History Trail. "Trelawny Building." https://pmwht.org.

Public Theatre. "Our Story." https://thepublictheatre.org.

Reilly, Wayne E. *Hidden History of Bangor: From Lumbering Days to the Progressive Era*. Dover, NH: Arcadia Publishing, 2013.

———. "Where Was the Devil's Half Acre?" *Bangor Daily News*, September 16, 2012. www.bangordailynews.com.

Rich, Nathaniel, and Christopher Lehmann-Haupt. "Stephen King, the Art of Fiction No. 189." *Paris Review* 178, Fall 2006. www.theparisreview.org.

Robbins, Ryan R. "The Brady Gang." Bangor In Focus. http://bangorinfo.com.

Rogak, Lisa. *Haunted Heart: The Life and Times of Stephen King*. New York: St. Martin's Publishing Group, 2010.

Rose, Charlie. Interview with Stephen King. "Charlie Rose." PBS. 1993. https://youtu.be/X0Pm5LB4aDs?si=x8tprIq61XpXsp_n.

"Rumford Comprehensive Plan." Prepared by Androscoggin Valley Council of Governments. November 1998. https://rumfordme.org.

Singer, Mark. "What Are You Afraid Of." *New Yorker*, August 30, 1998. www.newyorker.com.

Spignesi, Stephen. *The Complete Stephen King Encyclopedia: The Definitive Guide to the Works of America's Master of Horror*. Chicago: Contemporary Books, 1991.

Staff, Maine Campus. "Maine Campus March 05 1970." (1970). Maine Campus Archives. 513. https://digitalcommons.library.umaine.edu/.

———. "Maine Campus March 12 1970" (1970). Maine Campus Archives. 514. https://digitalcommons.library.umaine.edu.

———. "Maine Campus March 26 1970" (1970). Maine Campus Archives. 515. https://digitalcommons.library.umaine.edu.

Stephen King official website. "Cujo." https://stephenking.com.

Stenberg, Henry G. "A Study of Maine Central Railroad Passenger Service Since 1900." (1965). Electronic Theses and Dissertations. 3543. https://digitalcommons.library.umaine.edu/etd/3543.

The Strathglass Park Preservation Society. http://strathglass.org.

Sun Journal. "Pain of Deadly Accident Still Resonates Year Later." May 11, 2005. www.sunjournal.com.

University of Maine. *Prism Yearbook* 73, no. 23 (1970).

———. University Photograph Archive, Raymond H. Fogler Library Special Collections Department, University of Maine, Orono, Maine.

U.S. Census Bureau. "Population of Maine by Counties 1950." www2.census.gov.

Vincent, Bev. *Stephen King: A Complete Exploration of His Work, Life, and Influences*. Edwardsville, IL: Epic Ink, 2022.

Watkins, Ambra S. "Lisbon High's Most Celebrated Alumnus." *Lisbon Monthly*, November 1986.

Wendell, Bryan. "So Cool It's Scary: Stephen King References Scouting in More than Half of His Novels." Aaron on Scouting. Boy Scouts of America. August 19, 2020. https://blog.scoutingmagazine.org.

ABOUT THE AUTHOR

Sharon Kitchens has lived in Maine for a couple decades. She has written about food and agriculture for a variety of New England publications. Every week she can be seen carrying an armload of library books. She loves hanging out in cafés eating chocolate croissants and sipping lavender lattes. Her fondness for Patti Smith's poetry is matched only by her love of Taylor Swift's lyrics. She is a cat and dog person. She recently started a Substack newsletter: https://deliciousmusings.substack.com.

Visit us at
www.historypress.com